The Fate of White America

The Fate of
White America

Constantin von Hoffmeister

Multipolar Press
2026

THE FATE OF WHITE AMERICA

First edition

Published by Multipolar Press

multipolarpress.com

ISBN: 978-1-970784-13-8

Contents

1. The Crisis of White America

This chapter examines the transformation of the American nation through the lens of identity, demography, and historical continuity. It revisits early twentieth-century diagnoses of civilizational strain and places them within the present, where questions once considered peripheral have returned to the center of national life.

The American lawyer, conservationist, and amateur anthropologist Madison Grant (1865–1937), writing in the early twentieth century amid the massive immigration waves that transformed the United States between the 1880s and the First World War, offered a grim assessment of what he believed threatened the ethnic and cultural foundations of the American republic. In his influential and controversial book *The Passing of the Great Race* (1916), Grant argued that the strength of the nation grew from what he described as its "race consciousness": the heritage, temperament, and ethnocultural inheritance carried by the early settlers of British and Northern European origin who established the colonies and later built the American republic. Grant placed his argument within a broader historical narrative stretching from Tacitus's descriptions of the Germanic tribes to the Anglo-Saxon migrations and the Protestant settlers who crossed the Atlantic in the seventeenth century. From his perspective, the vitality of the United States resembled the organic growth of earlier civilizations, an idea present in the historical philosophy of Thomas

Carlyle and later systematized in the civilizational analyses of Oswald Spengler. Today, that foundation appears increasingly strained as demographic change accelerates transformations that Grant already feared a century ago. Paleontologist Henry Fairfield Osborn's admonishment, in his preface to Grant's book, delivered in language that startled readers of his time, now reads with renewed urgency:

> Thus conservation of that race which has given us the true spirit of Americanism is not a matter either of racial pride or of racial prejudice; it is a matter of love of country, of a true sentiment which is based upon knowledge and the lessons of history rather than upon the sentimentalism which is fostered by ignorance. If I were asked: What is the greatest danger which threatens the American republic today? I would certainly reply: The gradual dying out among our people of those hereditary traits through which the principles of our religious, political and social foundations were laid down and their insidious replacement by traits of less noble character.

For Grant, this phenomenon represented far more than a simple cultural adjustment between the newcomers and the host society. He saw in it the slow unraveling of an ancestral inheritance that had shaped the American experiment since the days of Jamestown and Plymouth.

Grant maintained that the problem extended far beyond the mere counting of populations. For him, the deeper struggle concerned the preservation of ideals, traditions, and habits of character that distinguished the American civilization created by the founding generation. When he wrote about the "suicidal ethics" spreading through modern society, he referred to the moral climate emerging in the late nineteenth and early twentieth centuries, when universalist doctrines, cosmopolitan liberalism, and the rhetoric of abstract equality gained prestige in academic and political circles. Grant believed these ideas weakened the instinct of collective preservation among the native White population, whose ancestors had constructed the institutions of the republic through centuries of frontier struggle and industrial development. The immigrant multitudes arriving from southern and eastern Europe in Grant's day, and from other regions in later decades, often adopted the visible forms of American life: language, clothing, and public customs. Yet Grant insisted that the deeper principles of the American tradition, shaped by the Anglo-Protestant ethos and the political philosophy of the Founding Fathers, remained difficult to transmit through superficial imitation alone. The founders themselves had envisioned a republic grounded in the political rights of "free White men," drawing inspiration from classical antiquity, the English common law tradition, and the Protestant moral order. In Grant's interpretation, the true danger therefore arose from the complacency of White Americans themselves. While the demographic and cultural character of their country shifted before their eyes, many continued to promote ideologies and policies that hastened the dissolution of the very inheritance that had built the nation. Grant regarded this condition as a summons to vigilance: a call for White Americans to rediscover the ethnocultural legacy entrusted to them by earlier generations and to recognize the civilizational peril contained in the abandonment of collective self-preservation.

In the present age, the transformation of America resembles far less the harmonious fusion often celebrated under the metaphor of the "melting pot." Instead, the process increasingly resembles the dismantling of a once cohesive society that had long revolved around a dominant cultural center. Earlier waves of immigration did produce assimilation over time, partly because newcomers encountered a confident and assertive host culture that expected adaptation. The current situation looks different. Fragmentation rather than integration shapes the atmosphere of public life. Immigration policies that encourage large-scale entry from populations distant from the original founding stock have accelerated cultural and demographic change. The signs of strain appear in many directions: borders that function more as symbolic markers than as enforceable lines, cities divided into enclaves with diverging customs and loyalties, and political rhetoric that celebrates "diversity" while dissolving the older unity that once grew from a shared ethnocultural framework. The United States now drifts through a moment of demographic rebalancing in which the historical majority steadily loses its numerical weight. In the towns of the interior, where earlier generations raised flags for common principles and maintained communities bound by ancestry and memory, a different atmosphere prevails. Silence sometimes replaces confidence; discord sometimes replaces shared outlook. The shrinking of the White American majority therefore carries meaning beyond statistics. A void emerges where a unified American worldview once held sway, replaced by competing cultural blocs whose emotional centers of gravity often lie beyond the borders of the republic.

Along the southern frontier, this transformation appears in its most visible form. The border increasingly resembles a wound rather than a boundary, releasing waves of migration into a nation already struggling with internal strain. Illegal immigration, on a vast scale, reshapes the cultural and demographic structure of the country. Tens of millions arrive over time through channels that bypass formal assimilation. Their presence alters the cultural equilibrium rather than blending quietly into it. Criminal networks exploit the situation as well. Drug cartels operate across the borderlands, trafficking narcotics and human beings through corridors of profit and violence. At the same time, public institutions feel the pressure of rapid population growth: schools overflow with students from many linguistic backgrounds, hospitals confront constant overcrowding, and police departments attempt to maintain order within increasingly complex urban environments. In many regions, the infrastructure built for a smaller and more culturally uniform population struggles to cope with the new reality. Yet powerful voices within political and corporate elites continue to frame these developments as evidence of "moral progress" and "humanitarian enlightenment." This rhetoric masks a deeper transformation: the gradual replacement of the historical builders of the American nation with a population shaped more by global economic currents than by any rooted connection to the country's founding heritage.

The consequences appear most vividly in the American heartland, where the rural landscapes and small towns that once symbolized national stability now display the marks of decline. For generations, these communities thrived through large families, agricultural continuity, and networks of kinship that stretched across counties and states. Churches, schools, and local associations reinforced a shared sense of belonging grounded in ancestry and place. In recent decades, this structure weakened. Suicide rates climbed sharply, particularly among White Americans in middle age, turning self-destruction into one of the leading causes of death. Opioid addiction spread through towns where economic opportunity faded. In certain regions, life expectancy fell towards levels associated with third-world nations rather than a wealthy industrial republic. The old image of the United States as a land of boundless opportunity gradually gave way to scenes of boarded storefronts, abandoned houses, and "For Sale" signs, property purchased by investors, sometimes from abroad. The resulting vacuum resembles an internal implosion rather than an external conquest. Shared ideals, collective identity, and confidence in the future dissolve into an atmosphere of isolation and despair. A haunting historical parallel arises here. The American nation once expanded across the continent through the power of Anglo-American civilization, displacing the indigenous cultures of the American Indians through warfare, disease, alcohol dependency, forced relocation, and cultural dissolution. Liberal American identity replaced older tribal traditions. Now, in an ironic historical turn, that same culture distorter spreads across the broader population. The reservation once stood at the edge of the national map. In the contemporary environment, the reservation becomes a metaphor for the entire society. Large portions of the population inhabit zones of economic stagnation and cultural disorientation that resemble internal reservations scattered throughout the republic.

While the heartland weakens, the industrial backbone that once supported these communities also deteriorates. During the twentieth century, the United States rose to global prominence through massive industrial production. Steel mills in Pennsylvania, automobile factories in Michigan, textile plants in the Carolinas, and shipyards along both coasts generated wealth and pride for generations of workers. These industries also created social worlds of solidarity where families expected stable employment and local identity revolved around shared labor. The late twentieth century introduced a different trajectory. Globalization encouraged corporations to relocate production to regions where wages remained far lower and regulations looser. Political leaders celebrated the new international economic order as a triumph of efficiency and progress. Yet the consequences for many American towns proved devastating. Factories closed or relocated overseas, leaving behind hollow shells of brick buildings, rusting machines, and silent smokestacks. Entire communities lost the economic purpose that had sustained them for decades. Workers who once shaped steel, assembled automobiles, or built machinery for the global market suddenly found themselves displaced in an economy that valued financial speculation and service labor more than manufacturing skill. The disappearance of industry therefore removed more than paychecks. It erased the social structure that had given meaning to countless American lives.

Even as these transformations reshape the country, the political and economic elites who guide the machinery of global capitalism continue to operate from distant centers of power. From corporate boardrooms and government offices, they observe the consequences of globalization with a mixture of detachment and optimism. Financial markets thrive, multinational corporations expand their reach, and technological innovation promises ever greater productivity. Automation and artificial intelligence enter factories, offices, and transportation networks, replacing human labor at a pace faster than workers can retrain for new roles. The emerging gig economy fragments employment into temporary tasks: a delivery here, a freelance contract there, a patchwork of income streams lacking stability or long-term security. In official rhetoric, this transformation appears as the triumph of modern progress. For many citizens living through the upheaval, the experience feels different. Progress manifests as eviction notices, mounting debt, addiction, and a sense that the economic order has left them behind. Technology once hailed as the instrument of liberation now deepens their marginalization, transforming them into spectators within an economic system that values efficiency over community. In this atmosphere, the promise of innovation coexists with a widening cultural vacuum. The myth of progress continues to glow in the language of policymakers and media commentators, while on the ground countless Americans confront a reality of displacement, uncertainty, and fading national confidence.

The narrative of Grant's work draws forth a vision of the swirling maelstrom of racial intermingling, not unlike the transcendent terror that is the eternal war among the Great Old Ones, their inscrutable conflicts shaping the universe's very fabric. Grant details the Nordic race's travels, its encounters with other groups, and the consequent racial blends that arise. This, according to Grant, has led to the gradual dilution and potential disappearance of the pure Nordic bloodline: a passing of the Great Race, as he ominously foretells.

Grant, through the lens of his morbid fascination, views this racial intermingling as a doom, an encroaching darkness threatening to snuff out the pure flame of the Nordic race. A doom evoking that which the mad Arab Abdul Alhazred prophesied in the unholy *Necronomicon*: the awakening of the slumbering Great Old Ones, destined to reduce our mortal realm to a screaming pandemonium under an alien sky.

Grant was not content to let this grim prognosis rest unchallenged. The prophesied awakening of the Great Old Ones may yet be forestalled by arcane rites and brave souls. In a similar vein, Grant posited a salvation for the Nordic race. He championed a rigid system of eugenics, a ghoulish protocol aimed to perpetuate the purity of the Nordic lineage, thereby preserving the civilization it had begotten. It was a dire prescription, emanating from the depths of Grant's concern for the welfare of his kinsmen.

In essence, *The Passing of the Great Race* is a volume of deep anthropological concern, scribed by a man driven by fears for his race's survival, mirroring those hapless souls who stand vigil against the awakening of cosmic horrors. As the moon casts long, eerie shadows upon a decaying necropolis, Grant's call for the Nordic race's conservation seems to reverberate through the epochs, a chilling dirge for a race he perceives on the brink of extinction. It is a testament to the same unnerving dance with destiny that each entity within H. P. Lovecraft's pantheon must contend with: an eternal struggle against inevitable dissolution, under the cold, indifferent gaze of a universe teetering on the edge of chaotic oblivion.

Oswald Spengler, a man renowned for his prophetic visions of societal decay, might well have beheld *The Passing of the Great Race* with a weary, knowing gaze. Having penned *The Decline of the West* (1918-1922), a grand chronicle of the cyclical rise and fall of cultures, Spengler would have scoffed at Grant's simplistic focus on the preservation of racial purity. To Spengler's cultured understanding, civilizations rise and wane, not from the commingling of races but from a metaphysical ebb and flow, a cultural metamorphosis as inevitable as the awakening of Lovecraft's dreaded Old Ones from their eons-old slumber. Comparable to the fatalistic threads of Lovecraft's cosmic tapestry binding every creature to an inescapable destiny, Spengler too would contend that civilizations, Nordic or otherwise, are bound by an inexorable fate, their decline as certain as the dusk that follows the day's fleeting light.

Just as Lovecraft's fiction is oftentimes concerned with great entities relegated to the shadows by time's relentless march, Spengler perceived in the narrative of racial purity not the path to salvation but the death knell of a civilization grappling against the inevitable drift of decline. To him, this focus on race, like the arcane obsession of Abdul Alhazred with the Great Old Ones, was a futile attempt to stave off an inescapable destiny, a struggle as hopeless as that of mortal men against the evil lurking in the interstices of time and space. Spengler might have gazed upon Grant's work as one gazes upon the non-Euclidean geometry of R'lyeh, an enigma fraught with despair, misunderstanding, and an unknowable dread, the dire prognosis of a race not in its physical extinction but in its inability to comprehend the profound cyclical ebb of cultural tides.

In the shadowed hush of a long-abandoned oak-paneled study lined with dusty trophies of vanished megafauna and yellowed maps of the unspoiled West, old Madison Grant rose like a spectral sentinel from his leather chair, his patrician features hardened into a mask of cold, ancestral fury as he seized my arm with fingers still strong from years of mountain trails and big-game rifles. "They smear my name as if it were a curse," he growled, his voice a deep, resonant timbre echoing like the last clean wind across untainted prairies, "yet in *The Passing of the Great Race* I laid bare the hideous truth they dare not face: the ancient Nordic stock—the tall, fair, clear-eyed builders who conquered the wilderness, raised the Republic from virgin soil, and gave the world its highest expressions of law and liberty—is being steadily erased from the continent it tamed. I saw the flood coming: the endless tide of lesser breeds from southern Europe, the Alpine round-heads, the Mediterranean swarms, and beyond them the Asiatic and African masses pouring through every opened gate, diluting the vital germ-plasm that once pulsed with the fire of explorers and empire founders. I warned that without iron barriers, without the sacred duty of preservation and selection, this Great Race would pass not in a heroic sunset but in a squalid twilight of mongrel chaos, its cathedrals turned to Babel, its cities to teeming warrens, its very bloodline dissolved into the formless, staring ocean of the unfit, until the last true American awakens to find himself a stranger in the land his fathers wrested from savagery, gazing upon a nightmare where the omen of replacement has already claimed the future!"

2. The Emergence of the White American

This chapter traces the historical formation of "Whiteness" in the American context, not as an ancient inheritance but as a product of colonial conditions, settlement, and political necessity. It explores how disparate European identities converged into a single category that shaped the social and institutional foundations of the republic.

The concept of "Whiteness" emerged gradually during the early centuries of European expansion into the Americas, especially during the seventeenth century when settlers from various regions of Europe encountered populations whom they perceived as radically different in appearance, language, and culture. English colonists in Virginia and New England, Dutch traders in New Netherland, Spanish administrators in the Caribbean, and French settlers along the St. Lawrence all confronted the same phenomenon: the presence of indigenous peoples and later enslaved Africans whose existence forced Europeans to define themselves collectively in new ways. Out of these encounters grew a broad racial designation that grouped together many European ethnicities beneath a single umbrella identity. Englishmen, Germans, Scots-Irish, Swedes, and other arrivals who had once carried distinct loyalties and regional traditions gradually found themselves categorized together as "White." This identity developed through colonial laws, social practices, and economic systems that separated European settlers from the indigenous populations they displaced and from the enslaved Africans whose labor sustained plantation economies. Through this process, the colonial societies of North America constructed a hierarchy that placed Europeans at the summit, laying the institutional foundations for racial stratification in the emerging American order. The category of "Whiteness" therefore functioned less as a description of ancient identity than as a newly forged political instrument shaped by the conditions of conquest, settlement, and labor exploitation in the New World.

The embrace of this racial category carried a deeper cultural consequence: it required settlers to loosen their attachment to the many European identities they had carried across the Atlantic. In the early decades of colonization, communities still preserved strong connections to their ancestral homelands. German-speaking farmers in Pennsylvania maintained their dialects and religious traditions, Swedish settlers along the Delaware River preserved Lutheran customs from Scandinavia, and English colonists continued to replicate the social structures and parish life of the British Isles. Over time, however, the growing pressure to maintain unity among settlers in a frontier environment encouraged the development of a simplified identity that transcended these older distinctions. The label "White" gradually overshadowed older affiliations rooted in language, region, and confession. This development did not erase European traditions entirely, yet it encouraged a broader sense of solidarity among settlers who otherwise differed in background. By adopting this collective identity, colonists created a framework that strengthened cooperation against populations they perceived as external or hostile. In practical terms, this simplification eased governance within the colonies and reinforced systems of authority that relied upon a clear separation between ruling and subordinate groups. The new identity thus served strategic purposes. It forged cohesion among disparate settlers while simultaneously reinforcing the racial boundaries that underpinned colonial domination.

This process of simplification also intersected with the intellectual climate that eventually produced the American Revolution. By the eighteenth century, Enlightenment ideas circulated widely among colonial elites, encouraging concepts of universal rights, civic equality among citizens, and representative government. Political pamphlets and sermons invoked themes drawn from classical republicanism and British constitutionalism, shaping the ideological language of the revolutionary generation. Within this environment, the notion of a unified White population supported the emerging vision of a shared political community among European settlers. The revolutionary leaders who declared independence in 1776 envisioned a republic composed of citizens who could see themselves as members of a single polity, liberated from the hierarchical structures associated with European aristocracy. The racial category of "Whiteness" therefore aligned with the leveling impulse embedded in revolutionary rhetoric. It allowed colonists of varied European backgrounds to imagine themselves as equals within a new democratic order while still maintaining a boundary that separated them from indigenous nations and enslaved Africans. In this sense, the consolidation of European identities into a single racial category mirrored the broader ideological transformation of the age. The flattening of older ethnic distinctions reflected the liberal revolutionary ethos that sought to redefine relations among individuals, communities, and political authority in the young American republic, forging a new civic identity that rested upon the shared designation of "white citizens" within the emerging national state.

In the half-light of a crumbling colonial library, where

yellowed broadsides curled like dead skin and the faint scent of gunpowder still lingered in the bindings, old Elias Thorne clutched my sleeve with trembling fingers that carried the chill of Valley Forge winters and fixed me with eyes burning with unearthly fervor. "Listen well, for few dare speak it aloud," he rasped, his voice a low, grating wind sweeping across blood-soaked battlefields, "after 1776, from the shattered husk of British colonies, there arose something new and terrible under heaven: the White American—not merely an Englishman abroad, but a distinct and higher breed created in the furnace of independence, a tall, restless, Nordic-Saxon stock tempered by frontier hardship, Puritan fire, and the clear-eyed genius of liberty. From the yeoman farmers of New England, the Scotch-Irish warriors of the Appalachians, the Cavalier planters of Virginia, and the sturdy German stock of Pennsylvania there coalesced a people who claimed the continent as their birthright, taming wilderness with axe and rifle, raising republics where once only forests stood, and declaring to the watching stars that this new race would brook no king, no ancient yoke, and no dilution of its blood. They were the rightful heirs of the Great Race, bold conquerors who carried the torch of Western civilization westward in a divine surge of expansion and creation."

3. *Paleface* and the Melting Pot

This chapter engages with Wyndham Lewis's critique of modern Western conscience and the ideology of the melting pot. Through satire and philosophical reflection, it examines the moral paradox of a civilization that expanded across the globe while cultivating an ethical framework that increasingly questions its own legitimacy.

Wyndham Lewis's *Paleface: The Philosophy of the Melting Pot* burst into the world in 1929, born in the interwar years when Europe still carried the scars of the Great War and the intellectual climate of the West simmered with anxiety about race, civilization, and the future of the modern world. The trenches of the Somme and Verdun had consumed millions of European lives only a decade earlier, and the old confidence of Western civilization stood shaken. Writers and philosophers across the continent searched for explanations. Oswald Spengler had already published *The Decline of the West*, proclaiming the twilight of Faustian civilization, while political movements from Bolshevism to Fascism attempted to reorganize societies shattered by war. Into this charged atmosphere, Lewis launched his book like a steel projectile. His argument unfolded through satire, provocation, and philosophical reflection. He declared that the destiny of the White man must be read through the example of America, a vast social laboratory where the peoples of Europe mingled with populations from every continent. The United States became for Lewis a mirror in which Europe could glimpse its own racial future: indigenous peoples pushed aside, Black populations brought through slavery, Asian migration rising along the Pacific rim, and a White population struggling to define its place in a rapidly changing world. In Lewis's interpretation, this situation created a profound moral drama. The White man's position appeared unstable, burdened by the legacy of conquest and empire. Every historical action carried a moral reckoning, every victory produced a new wave of guilt, and the entire civilization seemed haunted by the voice of a Puritan preacher demanding repentance and sacrifice.

Lewis began his meditation with the problem of conscience, which he treated as one of the defining psychological forces of modern Western civilization. For him, the moral intensity of Protestant culture produced chains heavier than iron or artillery. Protestant nations had marched into history with the Bible in one hand and the sword in the other. They subdued indigenous peoples across continents, built colonial empires stretching from Africa to Asia, and organized global trade networks that reshaped the world economy. Yet, after centuries of expansion, the same societies turned inward, judging themselves through an ever more severe moral lens. Lewis described this transformation with biting irony. The conqueror who once celebrated victory now bowed in contrition before the conquered. In this psychological reversal, guilt began to operate like a new religion. The White skin that earlier generations treated as a symbol of triumph became, in Lewis's satirical depiction, a badge of shame worn before the tribunal of modern morality. Lewis ridiculed academic racial science that measured skulls and cataloged physical features in the hope of proving superiority. His laughter carried a darker implication: the moral authorities of Western culture had already condemned their own civilization. The priests of conscience had blackened the spirit of the White world more effectively than any external enemy.

In Lewis's imaginative framework, the Indian, the "Redskin" of American frontier mythology, appeared as a kind of philosophical counterexample. He asked readers to imagine a reversed world in which indigenous peoples held global power. In such a world, copper skin would shine with sacred prestige. Laws would celebrate Choctaw or Blackfoot superiority, and poets would compose hymns to the virtues of tribal ancestry. Racial pride would exist as an unquestioned fact of social life, just as it had existed in many historical civilizations from ancient Sparta to imperial China. Lewis used this speculation to advance a larger claim: racial consciousness existed in nearly every society except the modern West, whose moral introspection dissolved the instinct of collective pride. Through the pressure of conscience, the White man alone permitted doubt to corrode the sense of belonging rooted in ancestry and culture.

Lewis then turned his argument towards philosophy itself. He examined the ethical theories of the British idealist T. H. Green, whose thought drew heavily from Hegelian philosophy and exerted considerable influence upon late Victorian liberalism. Green's moral vision emphasized duty, universal brotherhood, and the infinite responsibility each individual owed to the wider community of mankind. Lewis presented this philosophy as the culmination of a long moral evolution within Western thought. Classical Greek culture, in his portrayal, celebrated beauty, proportion, and the harmonious development of mind and body. Christian moralism introduced a different orientation. It elevated renunciation, humility, and self-sacrifice as supreme virtues. Through Protestantism, these ideas intensified further, encouraging individuals to surrender personal pleasure and even collective interest in the name of abstract humanitarian ideals. Lewis argued that this inheritance placed Europe in a paradoxical position. The

civilization that built empires across the globe simultaneously cultivated an ethical system that condemned power
itself. In sacrificing its own vitality to the altar of universal
morality, Europe risked transforming strength into decay.

Lewis called this paradox the "moral situation." In
such a world, ethical ideals multiplied endlessly, demanding constant acts of renunciation from individuals and societies alike. The result resembled an atmosphere thick with
righteousness. Men struggled beneath impossible expectations, each new moral demand adding weight to the burden
already placed upon their shoulders. Through this fog of
duty, another idea emerged in Lewis's thinking: the notion
of *esprit de peau*, the "spirit of skin." By this phrase, he
meant the instinctive solidarity that binds communities
through shared ancestry and appearance. Throughout history, many societies defended privilege through visible
markers of belonging. Ancient Greek city-states reserved
citizenship for those born within the civic body. Brahmin
castes in India guarded ritual and social authority through
hereditary status. Where privilege weakened, Lewis argued,
racial cohesion also declined. He pointed to the history of
European Jewry as an example of transformation. Once
burdened by stigma and exclusion, Jewish communities
gradually achieved recognition through intellectual and
economic accomplishment. For Lewis, this demonstrated
that racial categories operated within shifting structures of
power and prestige. When privilege vanished, the dominant race itself risked dissolving into an anonymous mass
of interchangeable laborers serving the machinery of modern industry.

From this observation, Lewis introduced the figure
of the outlaw, a symbolic type representing the natural
leaders of the Western world who now found themselves
excluded from authority. In earlier eras, aristocracies, warrior castes, and cultural elites provided direction to their

societies. In the modern age, according to Lewis, such figures drifted towards the margins. Political institutions and moral doctrines stripped them of legitimacy. The law they once embodied collapsed beneath democratic leveling and bureaucratic uniformity. These displaced figures wandered like prophets whose warnings fell upon deaf ears. They perceived the possibility that Western civilization might gradually merge into broader global systems, losing its distinct character in the process. Lewis compared their predicament to the tragic figure of Cassandra from Greek mythology, whose accurate prophecies earned ridicule rather than belief.

Lewis also launched an attack upon what he called the "cult of the primitive." Literary culture in the 1920s often celebrated supposed vitality in non-European societies. Writers such as Sherwood Anderson, D. H. Lawrence, and the young Ernest Hemingway explored themes of instinct, blood consciousness, and primal authenticity. Jazz rhythms, African sculpture, and indigenous spirituality fascinated many modern artists who sought an escape from the perceived sterility of industrial civilization. Lawrence, for instance, described Whites as creatures of spirit yearning to reconnect with deeper biological forces. Anderson's novel *Dark Laughter* romanticized the supposed vitality of Black American culture. Lewis regarded this fascination as a dangerous illusion. In his view, Western intellectuals praised the energy of other cultures while dismissing the achievements of their own. This posture encouraged self-denigration and spiritual exhaustion. Lewis even pointed to rising rates of student suicide as evidence of psychological disorientation among young Europeans exposed to narratives of civilizational decline.

Lewis sharpened his satire through the language of psychology. Modern society, he argued, distributed complexes like ideological gifts. Whites received an inferiority complex that undermined confidence in their own traditions. Blacks and other groups received a superiority complex encouraged by liberal rhetoric celebrating their supposed "authenticity" and "vitality." The social order thus underwent a symbolic inversion in which the historical masters of Western civilization became objects of condemnation. Lewis mocked the fashionable fascination with Freud, sexual neuroses, and sentimental introspection that dominated much of modern literature. Sentimentality, in his critique, weakened the cultural will. Sentimental primitivism, sentimental sexuality, and sentimental politics all contributed to a climate where emotional indulgence replaced disciplined thought. In such an atmosphere, societies lost the intellectual clarity necessary for survival.

Behind this cultural drama could be heard the roaring machinery of the industrial age. Lewis observed that technological civilization created its own contradictions. Factories, assembly lines, and mechanized warfare transformed the economic and social structure of the West. The White worker increasingly became a component within vast industrial systems. At the same time, intellectual circles dreamed nostalgically about noble savages and tribal authenticity. Lewis ridiculed this schizophrenia. Class struggle and racial anxiety intersected within the same industrial environment. Machines devoured both, reducing human beings to units of labor measured by efficiency and productivity. Despite this bleak picture, Lewis refused simple despair. He called for a new philosophical orientation grounded in intellectual rigor rather than sentimental fantasy, a renewed understanding of Western civilization capable of confronting the realities of the modern world.

Lewis provocatively proposed "a model melting pot." The phrase deliberately echoed the famous metaphor popularized by the Jewish playwright Israel Zangwill, whose 1908 drama *The Melting Pot* celebrated the assimilation of immigrants into a unified American identity. Lewis seized the concept and reshaped it for his own purposes. The White world, he argued, required unity through internal fusion rather than dissolution through indiscriminate mixture. The peoples of Europe—Swiss peasants, Swedish villagers, English farmers, German workers—shared deep cultural and historical affinities. Yet national rivalries encouraged them to slaughter one another in catastrophic wars. The First World War revealed the absurdity of these divisions. Brothers blinded brothers with poison gas; cousins annihilated cousins with artillery. Lewis concluded that Europe required a broader political and civilizational unity, a melting pot composed of related peoples rather than unrelated strangers.

Lewis envisioned a continental transformation resembling what had occurred in the United States, where Germans, Irish, Italians, and many other European groups gradually merged into a broader American identity. He ridiculed narrow nationalism that clung to provincial rivalries inherited from earlier centuries. For Lewis, the White man faced a stark choice: transcend national fragmentation or confront extinction through endless fratricidal conflict. The catastrophe of the Great War nearly destroyed the European race. Another war on a similar scale could complete the process. Only a unified European *imperium*—a melting pot of kin bound by shared heritage—could preserve the civilization that emerged from the ancient Greeks, the Roman Empire, and the Christian Middle Ages.

Lewis's argument resonated strongly with the warnings issued by Oswald Spengler, who observed that non-European societies had mastered Western technology and military techniques, thereby challenging the global dominance once enjoyed by Europe. Lewis echoed this concern. Fortress isolation could not protect Europe indefinitely. The world pressed inward through economic competition, migration, and cultural exchange. The White world therefore required unity to face the global tide as a coherent bloc rather than as fragmented nations competing against one another.

Throughout *Paleface, Lewis* balanced irony with conviction. He mocked intellectual fashions even while advancing his own provocative conclusions. Contradictions surfaced deliberately within his rhetoric, reflecting his belief that satire often revealed truths concealed by solemn discourse. Yet the central message remained unmistakable: Western civilization must regain consciousness of itself. Self-knowledge and solidarity formed the prerequisites for survival in an increasingly turbulent global environment.

The legacy of *Paleface* remains contested. Many readers interpret the book as an unapologetic racial man-ifesto. Others read it as a satirical critique of primitivism and modern intellectual fashions. Whatever interpretation one adopts, the text occupies a distinctive place within the intellectual ferment of the interwar period. Lewis treated ideas as weapons capable of reshaping entire civiliza-tions. Philosophies, moral doctrines, and cultural myths possessed the power to destroy societies as effectively as armies and artillery. The danger facing the White world, in Lewis's view, emerged as much from internal ideas—guilt, sentimentalism, and ideological confusion—as from exter-nal rivals.

Lewis concluded with a sweeping historical specula-tion. If European civilization had remained isolated from the wider world, the global landscape might have evolved along entirely different lines. African societies might have developed along their own trajectories beside the Niger River. Indigenous tribes in North America might have con-tinued their nomadic pursuits across the plains. Europe might have preserved its internal strength in a manner comparable to the cultural continuity of China. Yet such isolation belonged to the realm of imagination. History advanced through dreams, exaggerations, and utopian visions that eventually hardened into reality.

At the edge of modern history, Lewis imagined Western civilization as a powerful machine standing upon uncertain ground. The challenge he posed still persists across the decades: whether Western civilization would gather its scattered energies and reshape its destiny, or whether the forces of fragmentation would carry it towards dissolution in the wider currents of global history.

4. America in the Multipolar Age

This chapter situates the United States within the emerging multipolar order, interpreting the shift away from unipolar dominance as a transformation rather than a disappearance of power. It considers how strategic retrenchment and internal consolidation may redefine the American role in a world of competing civilizations.

Multipolarity does not herald the disappearance of the United States from the stage of history. It signals a transformation in scale, ambition, and orientation. For more than a century, American power expanded outward with astonishing velocity. After the Spanish–American War of 1898, the republic stepped beyond continental boundaries, establishing influence across the Caribbean and Pacific. The Second World War elevated the United States into the central pillar of the Western alliance, and the collapse of the Soviet Union in 1991 seemed to grant Washington an unprecedented moment of global predominance. Political thinkers spoke of a "unipolar moment," an era when American institutions, economic models, and military alliances would shape the destiny of the planet. Multipolarity alters that trajectory. It implies that the United States gradually relinquishes the ambition of universal management and accepts a position among several major civilizational centers. America remains powerful, influential, and culturally vibrant, yet its energies turn inward towards national renewal. The country shrinks strategically rather than disappearing politically, concentrating its resources upon internal cohesion instead of planetary supervision. In this sense, multipolarity invites the United States to rediscover an older tradition visible in earlier periods of its history, when statesmen such as George Washington and John Quincy Adams warned against entangling the republic in endless foreign struggles.

The movement towards a more restrained American posture therefore arises less from deliberate doctrine than from a deeper historical reflex. Empires throughout history eventually confront the limits of expansion. Rome discovered those limits along the Rhine and the Euphrates; Spain felt them in the draining wars of the seventeenth century, and Britain recognized them after the exhaustion of two world wars. The American political body now exhibits similar symptoms of fatigue. Military interventions stretching from Vietnam and Iraq to Afghanistan and Iran imposed enormous financial and psychological burdens upon the nation. Trillions of dollars vanished into distant battlefields while domestic infrastructure aged and communities across the country struggled with economic dislocation. Under such pressure, a collective instinct of self-preservation begins to operate. Isolationism in this context emerges not as an ideological program drafted by strategists but as a practical reaction from a society weary of endless engagement. The United States turns its gaze inward, examining the fractures within its own civic structure. The dismantling of a far-flung imperial posture removes distractions that long diverted attention from internal decay. Through this process, the nation begins the difficult work of reconstruction, gathering the scattered pieces of its own historical foundation.

The order that emerges from such a transformation would differ markedly from earlier visions of global dominance. Twentieth-century strategists often imagined the

United States as a modern Rome, an imperial center radiating power through military bases, financial institutions, and cultural influence across every continent. Multipolarity dissolves that imperial aspiration. The United States becomes one pole among several powerful civilizations that shape the international system. China consolidates its position across East Asia and Eurasia. Russia asserts its geopolitical identity across the vast northern landmass. India develops its own civilizational trajectory within the Indian Ocean world. Europe continues its complex experiment with supranational institutions and regional integration. Within this constellation, America adopts a more focused identity. Its political culture grows leaner and more pragmatic, guided less by universal missionary zeal and more by the sober recognition of limits. Such a transformation may resemble the strategic realism advocated by earlier American thinkers who emphasized balance of power rather than ideological crusades. In a multipolar environment, the United States seeks stability through coexistence rather than domination.

Within this framework, the internal composition of the American nation also gains renewed importance. The historical core of the country, the founding stock—descendants of the European settlers who established the early republic—undergoes profound demographic and cultural transformation during the twenty-first century. Yet this population remains an integral component of the national story. Even amid social upheaval and demographic change, it retains a reservoir of historical memory that stretches back to the colonial settlements, the frontier experience, the Civil War, and the industrial rise of the nineteenth century. In a period of national reorientation, that legacy may provide a foundation for reconstruction. Cultural traditions rooted in the Anglo-American experience—legal institutions, constitutional government, Protestant ethical habits, and the ethos of frontier self-reliance—continue to shape American identity even as the broader population grows increasingly diverse. The rediscovery of these roots could serve as an anchor during the transition from imperial over-stretch to national consolidation.

Multipolarity therefore represents more than a shift in international alignments. It offers the United States an opportunity for rebirth through strategic humility. By abandoning the expectation of universal leadership, the nation frees itself from the illusions that accompanied decades of global intervention. Domestic renewal becomes possible once the machinery of empire relinquishes its grip upon the national imagination. Infrastructure, industry, community life, and cultural cohesion receive attention that previously flowed outward towards foreign commitments. In this environment, the United States learns to operate within a world of several great powers rather than a hierarchy dominated by one. Cooperation and competition replace unilateral command as the normal patterns of international politics.

Seen from this perspective, multipolarity appears less as a decline than as a maturation of the global system. History seldom permits any single civilization to dominate indefinitely. Instead, the world evolves through shifting constellations of power in which multiple cultures pursue their own trajectories. For the United States, the acceptance of this reality could open a path towards renewed authenticity. Stripped of imperial burdens, the nation confronts the raw materials of its own history: its traditions, contradictions, and possibilities. From these elements, a new American identity may gradually emerge, defined less by planetary ambition and more by the determination to thrive as one sovereign civilization among several.

5. White as a Marker

This chapter reflects on the meaning of identity in a cultural environment shaped by homogenizing forces. It explores how the term "White" functions not only as a racial designation but as a symbolic vessel for the preservation and continuity of inherited ethnocultural forms.

Racism lies with those who seek to diminish the value of racial belonging and consciousness, who disregard the ethnic identities who are actualized in the world's peoples. These groups aim to get rid of the particularity of races, reducing them to mere biological classifications, to superficial curiosities fit only for the pages of ethnographic studies. In doing so, they strip away the heritage that each race represents, transforming an invaluable aspect of the human species into something lifeless and trivial. The true threat to mankind lies not in the recognition of racial reality but in the deliberate attempt to ignore it.

It is those who twist the truth that would have us believe that acknowledging racial realities and the importance of ethnic identities leads inevitably to a xenophobic sense of superiority. Yet, in truth, it is not the recognition of differences that breeds contempt or hatred. Rather, these darker impulses arise in societies where the illusion of egalitarian coexistence obscures the natural distinctions between peoples. In such places as the United States, where racial identities are forcibly blended and denied their uniqueness, the seeds of resentment, superiority, and hatred are sown. True respect for others can only be built upon an understanding of difference, not the wiping out of it.

To be White in America is to carry a name formed across centuries of migration, settlement, and memory, a name shaped by Atlantic crossings, frontier clearings, and the slow weaving of European traditions into the landscape of a new continent. That identity travels through time like a quiet current. It moves through lullabies sung in farmhouses on winter nights, through hymns rising from wooden churches planted along colonial roads, through the stories families repeat at kitchen tables about ancestors who arrived with little more than faith, language, and stubborn endurance. European settlers brought with them fragments of old worlds: German chorales, English common law, Irish ballads, Scandinavian sagas, and French Catholic devotions. In America, these fragments mingled with the physical environment of forests, rivers, and open plains. Cathedrals became cornfields, monasteries became frontier chapels, yet the underlying spiritual memory endured. In the rustle of leaves in Appalachian woods or the quiet ring of a church bell across a Midwestern town, ancestral echoes persist. The word "White" gradually emerges as a vessel for that inheritance during moments when other labels lose their depth. The word "American," once charged with mythic meaning, sometimes appears in modern life as a hollow slogan printed on billboards or campaign banners. In such moments, another layer of identity awakens, something older and steadier. Within the word "White," an ancestral awareness stirs, neither defensive nor domineering, simply conscious of its own continuity.

True defiance against racism must rise from the recognition that the flame of ethnic consciousness and the truth of a people's identity are its rightful claim, to be acknowledged and honored by all, including its own kin. A people's right to its identity is not a hollow phrase; it demands the right to preserve its bloodline, the right to hold dominion over the land where its essence is strongest. Without sovereignty over the territory that belongs to its ancestral heritage, a people's identity is but a shadow, lost amidst the throngs of a vast plastic empire. When a folk is trapped within a sprawling political machine, surrounded by foreign tribes, and barred from mastery over its own land, its claim to identity fades like smoke in the wind. Only when ethnicity and territory are bound together under a people's rule can the right to existence be truly upheld by the sword and the shield.

In the present cultural climate, the doctrine commonly called "multiculturalism" operates in ways that dissolve the distinctive textures of inherited traditions. The policy language of diversity celebrates mixture and interchange, yet in practice the outcome sometimes resembles a solvent applied to historical identities. Customs that once possessed sacred resonance risk blending into a generic cultural atmosphere. Rituals, languages, and inherited patterns of life become interchangeable components in a universal mosaic. For individuals whose memory reaches back through European ancestors, this environment can generate a sense of dislocation. The structure of identity appears flooded by currents that blur boundaries rather than preserve them. Within that tide, the word "White" functions as a foothold. It offers a point of reference anchored in memory and cultural continuity. Through it, people recall songs, moral codes, architectural forms, and seasonal rhythms inherited from earlier generations. Identity therefore transforms into an act of devotion. It expresses love for origins, gratitude for the ancestors who carried traditions across centuries, and responsibility towards descendants who will inherit the cultural story.

Debates surrounding identity often confuse two distinct impulses. Supremacism speaks through the language of domination and hierarchy. Identity, in its more reflective form, speaks through the language of presence and belonging. A White American who rediscovers the meaning of his heritage does not necessarily pursue authority over others. Rather, he searches for a hearth, a center of gravity within a world that often rewards fragmentation and rootlessness. The metaphor of the hearth captures the essence of cultural loyalty. Around a hearth, families gather, stories circulate, and memory flows from elders to children. Such loyalty does not require hostility towards neighboring communities. Many thinkers describe this outlook through the concept of ethnopluralism, an arrangement in which different peoples cultivate their own traditions while respecting the space of others. In such a framework, the world resembles a garden composed of many species. Each flower grows through its own fragrance and rhythm, contributing to the broader harmony of the landscape.

In a world that seeks to impose uniformity, we must treasure the variety of human thought and expression. Attempts to impress a single pattern of thought upon the entire world would lead not to a forward movement but to stagnation. The vibrancy of human civilization comes from the multitude of ways in which different peoples have approached the fundamental questions of life and everything else. To impose one way of thinking, one system of values, upon all mankind would be to snuff out the creative spark that drives innovation and discovery. A world of uniformity is a world of death, where the rule of slow rot holds sway over the human spirit.

Within the American lexicon, the word "White" carries a resonance shaped by layers of history. It vibrates with the intellectual heritage of the Enlightenment, with the political imagination of Thomas Jefferson, with the musical architecture of Johann Sebastian Bach, with frontier hymns sung by settlers moving westward across mountains and prairies. It comes through in Viennese waltzes, Celtic chants, and the distant call of cavalry horns during nineteenth-century wars that defined the young republic. These references represent more than scattered cultural artifacts. Together, they form a frequency of memory, a shared tonal register through which many Americans interpret their place in the world. To identify as White within this context becomes a means of preserving that cultural frequency against the static of a society that sometimes reduces heritage to an optional curiosity. It affirms that the songs of earlier centuries still deserve to be sung in the present age, that memory requires breathing room within the modern cultural landscape.

Observers from Europe sometimes interpret the American usage of the term "White" as a purely racial designation. From their perspective, the label appears abstract, lacking the deep historical roots of national identities such as French, German, or Polish. Yet within the American environment, the term often functions as a cultural signal rather than a narrow biological category. The United States developed through waves of immigration that gradually blended distinct European peoples into a broader population. During the nineteenth and early twentieth centuries, immigrants from Ireland, Italy, Germany, and Eastern Europe absorbed themselves into an American mythos shaped by frontier expansion, industrial growth, and democratic politics. That mythos provided a common narrative for assimilation. In recent decades, the narrative itself has weakened. The shared story that once defined American belonging no longer commands universal allegiance. In the absence of that national mythology, the term "White" sometimes fills the vacuum as a new form of collective reference. It gathers fragments of ancestry and reconstructs them into a postmodern sense of kinship grounded less in state institutions than in ethnocultural affinities.

The word itself therefore undergoes a subtle transformation. Earlier generations sometimes used it carelessly or wielded it as a blunt instrument of exclusion. In the present moment, some individuals attempt to reshape the term through a process resembling cultural alchemy. They treat it as a sanctuary word, a symbol of remembrance rather than domination. Within that symbol lie intimate images: the village square in a European town, the tolling of a chapel bell across a valley, the quiet gaze of a grandmother whose stories connect living generations with forgotten ancestors. To utter the word "White" in this reflective sense involves tracing invisible maps of time and place. Those maps reveal migration routes from European villages to American farms, from crowded ports to frontier cabins, and from the memory of Old World traditions to the improvisations of New World life. Identity thus becomes a chronicle containing centuries of experience carried through bloodlines and cultural memory.

The affirmation of White identity aligns with a broader principle: the defense of distinct identities for all peoples. The difference between celebration and domination lies in the spirit that animates the affirmation. Celebration seeks harmony among cultures that respect each other's boundaries. Domination seeks hierarchy and control. A world stripped of cultural distinctions would produce only a uniform hum of administrative sameness, an environment managed through bureaucratic abstractions rather than lived traditions. A world composed of living cultures, by contrast, possesses texture, meaning, and historical depth. The affirmation of identity therefore becomes a promise. It promises that memory will endure through time, that inherited stories will continue to shape new generations, and that the manifold civilizations of the world will preserve their distinctive voices within the broader chorus of human history.

The word "White" gradually came to represent more than pigmentation. It served as a shorthand for a civilizational inheritance that included European philosophical traditions, Christian religious structures, classical music and literature, legal concepts drawn from Roman and English law, and the political ideals that animated the founding generation. When individuals employ the term in this context they often refer to the preservation of these intertwined cultural elements. The identification expresses a desire to maintain continuity with the values and traditions brought from Europe and adapted within the American landscape. It therefore functions less as a biological statement than as a symbolic defense against cultural erosion in an environment perceived as increasingly homogenizing.

The nature of existence itself is not absolute but relative, bound by the limitations of creation. Mankind's place in the universe is one of dependence and not autonomy. Our being is not self-sufficient. It is tied to forces beyond our control. This dependence is reflected in the very composition of our cultures, which are shaped by the environments in which we live and the histories we inherit. To deny this is to deny our own nature. Just as no individual can exist in isolation, neither can any culture stand alone, independent of the forces that shaped it. We are all, in the end, creatures of the world around us, bound by the laws of creation.

Gazing upon the churning maelstrom of the world today, we too are struck with awe and dread, as though peering into the heart of a nightmare. The instigators of global homogenization rage like a roaring red cauldron, consuming the uniqueness of cultures and ethnic identities in their path. Within this inferno, we witness entire peoples, like insects, fighting against an overwhelming tide, their ancestral ways crumbling beneath the weight of modernity and conformity. The flames of this destruction leap high into the sky, and above their deafening roar we hear the anguished cry of a dying ethnicity, a sound not of this earth but one that rings out from the distant abysses of forgotten time. This is the death cry of a vanishing race, the final scream of a culture once alive and exclusive, now being swallowed by the relentless advance of a world that seeks to make all things the same. As we listen to this inhuman wail, we are reminded that the fight to safeguard *authentic multiculturalism* is a battle for the spirit of mankind itself.

6. Blood on the Sand

This chapter turns to the frontier as a formative myth of American identity, examining the violence, expansion, and transformation that accompanied westward settlement. It considers how the memory of conquest continues to be active within the cultural and historical imagination of the nation.

Hagen von Tundra, a Faustian soul, tells a story of settlers who ventured straight into the heart of the untamed borderlands. They cut through grass, swamp, and plain, driven by a tide that turned westward. The blinding glare of the setting sun illuminated a heap of red corpses, setting the stage for the blood-boiling tale that was to unfold. Ashenfaced, with revolvers drawn and repeating rifles blazing, they fired down a desolate range, reclaiming the biosphere for noble treks that passed through icy winds at the break of dawn.

Remember the castle, besieged on all fronts. The wagon tents flapped in disgust at the invaders' nonchalance, their defiance a mere murmur against the savage beasts that roamed the land. *Kapow! Kapow!* Down went one feathered fellow, barely limping like a weakling in a worn and stolen saddle. "Presents then! And where now?" sounded the question through the wild expanse, where the bears were too wild and the women too tame, setting tables and preparing the hearth while the men were out there, planting and digging their own graves.

Generations yet unborn would gaze inward, reflecting their refinement, while ahead the landscape stretched onward. Do you smell the firewatered palms, upturned and begging for scraps? In the middle of this passionate heartland, there was a red-boiled rage to kill the reds, to scourge the country of its plague. Line by line, they designed a complex grid of lanes and trains to modernize, to civilize an ancient land steeped in evil intent. Through the mercy of God, they washed it clean, making it shine with a thousand skyscrapers piercing the clouds. And in their merciless advance, they never listened to the dead half-beast's cry, for theirs was a mission of divine destiny, a march to tame the wilderness and bring forth a new era of civilization.

Yet when the fires sank into embers and the rifles fell silent, a deeper murmur rose from the soil itself, and he spoke to me in a voice strained by some unseen pressure, "Do you think it ended with their victory?" I answered with uncertainty, for the land before us seemed altered in ways no tally of conquest could explain. "They believed they cleared it," I said, though the words felt thin, insufficient. He gave a slow, deliberate shake of the head. "Nothing is cleared," he replied. "Only covered. Only layered over with names, roads, and structures that pretend permanence." A wind moved across the plain, carrying with it a faint scent of burned meat and something older, something that clung beneath the surface of things. "Then what remains?" I asked, though even as I spoke I felt the answer pressing upward from below. He leaned closer, his eyes fixed upon the horizon where the last light faded into a dull, metallic haze. "Impressions," he said. "Residues of action, of violence, of will imposed and resisted. They settle into the ground, into memory, into the very arrangement of the world that follows." The silence deepened, thick, almost tangible, and for an instant I sensed that the vast grids of roads and towers, the shining surfaces of the cities, stood not as a final triumph, but as a thin and trembling layer stretched over something that had never yielded, something that waited in patience beneath the measured lines of progress, enduring every attempt to define it, to master it, to claim it as complete.

They rode westward beneath the blinding glare of a dying sun, piling red corpses like offerings to unseen gods, while the wagon tents flapped in silent disgust and the savage beasts of the old land roared their futile defiance; yet even as they scoured the earth of its ancient plague and laid down the iron grid of lanes and shining rails, they never heard the dead half-beast's final cry emanating from the soil they "civilized," for in that merciless advance the frontier was not closed; it was merely internalized, festering now within the soul of the machine-age republic, waiting to erupt again when the last illusions of refinement crumble and the skyscrapers themselves begin to scream!

In the brutal Indian Wars, settlers clashed with indigenous tribes. Blood and fire marked this dark epoch, as conflicts and massacres swept across the land. Entire tribes, like the Yuki in California, were driven to the brink of extinction. Amidst the chaos, the cycle of violence and displacement carved a path of destruction, underscoring the effects of a civilization bent on conquest and domination.

7. America's Faustian Spirit

This chapter interprets the United States through the lens of the Faustian impulse described by Oswald Spengler. It explores the drive towards expansion and innovation that has defined American civilization, from the conquest of the continent to the exploration of space.

In October 1916, at the very height of the First World War, when the armies of Europe were locked in mechanized slaughter across the trenches of the Somme, Verdun, and countless lesser-known killing fields, the young American writer H. P. Lovecraft paused to reflect upon the destiny of his own civilization. Europe's ancient nations—France, Germany, Britain, Austria-Hungary, and Russia—were consuming their youth in artillery barrages and poison gas clouds, an apocalypse that shattered the nineteenth century's confident faith in progress. Amid this upheaval, Lovecraft posed a stark question: "Do Americans desire to remain a vigorous, clean moraled Teutonic-Celtic people; or do they desire to transform their country into a sordid, amorphous chaos of degradation and hybridism like imperial Rome?" Lovecraft framed the issue through the lens of classical history. The Roman Empire, once disciplined and expansionist, had, in his view, degenerated into a cosmopolitan mass, where provincial peoples flooded the capital and the old Roman character dissolved. His question therefore went back to a much older debate about the fate of civilizations. Rome, Athens, Carthage, and later empires had all confronted moments when the identity that built them seemed to dissolve within the very universality they created. Lovecraft wondered whether America, barely a century and a half old, would follow the same trajectory.

For much of its early history, the United States understood itself as a civilization shaped primarily by European settlement. From the colonial era through the nineteenth century, the dominant cultural framework reflected the traditions of the British Isles and northern Europe, reinforced by the migration of Germans, Irish, Scandinavians, and other European peoples who gradually merged into the broader American population. Political leaders and intellectuals frequently described the nation as a continuation of Western civilization in the New World. That self-understanding began to shift dramatically during the twentieth century, particularly after the passage of the Immigration and Nationality Act of 1965, which replaced earlier quota systems that had favored European migration. The new legislation opened the doors of immigration more widely to Asia, Latin America, and other regions of the developing world. Over the following decades, the demographic composition of the United States changed at a pace unprecedented in the country's earlier history. More than sixty years after that legislative turning point, the question arises once again: how do White Americans themselves interpret the identity of the nation? In many regions of what journalists often call Middle America or "flyover country," large portions of the population still imagine the United States through the older narrative of a European-descended society. Migration patterns sometimes reflect this instinct for cultural continuity, as families relocate towards areas where communities retain familiar traditions and social norms. Yet the scale and speed of demographic change create a powerful countercurrent. For critics of contemporary immigration policy, merely slowing the influx appears insufficient. They argue that far-reaching measures would be necessary to restore the demographic balance that once defined the country's historical identity.

The broader historical significance of America, however, extends beyond demographic questions into the realm of civilizational character. Many observers have described the United States as an expression of the Faustian spirit identified by Oswald Spengler. In Spengler's analysis, the Faustian civilization of the West seeks endless expansion, exploration, and mastery over space. America embodies this impulse with remarkable intensity. The conquest of the American West during the nineteenth century illustrates the point vividly. Settlers crossed vast plains and mountain ranges, built railroads across deserts, and established cities where wilderness once stretched unbroken to the horizon. The frontier experience demanded willpower, endurance, and a willingness to confront the unknown. Through blood, sweat, and relentless determination, the expanding republic transformed an enormous continent into an industrial civilization. The same restless energy later propelled American achievements in science and technology. When the United States launched the Apollo and Mercury space programs during the Cold War, the symbolism reached far beyond the technical achievement of landing astronauts on the Moon. The missions carried the names of classical deities—Apollo, the radiant sun god, and Mercury, the swift messenger of Olympus—linking modern technological ambition with the mythological imagination of ancient Europe. The emblem of the eagle, long associated with imperial Rome and later adopted by the United States as its national symbol, seemed almost to reappear in a new form as rockets pierced the upper atmosphere. In that moment, the Promethean drive of Western civilization extended beyond the Earth itself.

This same civilizational temperament permeates

American culture on both practical and intellectual levels. The country's capitalist system encourages innovation, risk-taking, and the pursuit of ambitious projects that stretch the limits of human capability. Private enterprises increasingly carry forward the exploratory impulse that once belonged primarily to governments. Companies engaged in commercial space exploration attempt to push human presence deeper into the solar system, reviving the spirit that animated earlier national programs. In this sense, the descendants of Doctor Faustus, the legendary seeker of ultimate knowledge and power, continue their quest through the laboratories, launchpads, and research centers of modern America. The drive to transcend limits, to go farther and higher than previous generations imagined possible, remains deeply embedded within the American imagination.

There is no center. The center cannot hold. The cathedral has collapsed, but the scaffolding remains, a shrine to unfinished dreams. The stars are no longer divine. They are destinations. Telescopes replace prophets. Space becomes a product. Mars is the new Eden, except the serpent is a billionaire and the apple is a touchscreen. The Western soul clutches its mythology even as it repurposes it: Arthur in a business suit, Parsifal with a satellite uplink. T. S. Eliot called this "the hollow men," and he was right, but even hollow things resound. Nietzsche, flickering in and out like a bad transmission, mutters: "You killed God, yes, but now you haunt yourself. The abyss is inside you, and it keeps speaking in your voice."

The West dreams itself in fire, always fire, and names the blaze *progress*. It doesn't walk. It surges. Its pulse is Promethean, its bloodstream full of ancient ash. It writes manifestos with the bones of Heraclitus and quotes Milton with a straight face, even as it builds iPhones out of slave labor and cosmic loneliness. This is Faust, but with Wi-Fi.

This is Don Quixote, except the windmills are nuclear reactors and the tilting is algorithmic. The West stares into the mirror and sees Narcissus and Icarus kissing in the ruins of Carthage. Nietzsche watches this drama from the cheap seats of eternity, notes in hand, muttering: "You took my hammer and built a cathedral. You were supposed to smash the idols, not polish them."

The Faustian mind is a machine haunted by poetry. It cannot love without conquest. Even tenderness must be charted, dissected, reduced to graphs and theories. It sings, but the song becomes architecture, and the architecture becomes war. There is no rest, only projects. Every idea is a campaign. Every vision is a battlefield. Spengler saw this, called it civilizational morphology, but it's older than that: it's Gilgamesh refusing mortality, it's Hamlet talking himself into madness, it's Dante climbing out of Hell only to find he brought it with him. Nietzsche leans over our shoulder and snarls, "You built a heaven of intellect, but the gods you cast out have returned through the back door. You are possessed by what you tried to kill."

Literary culture reflects the same fascination with the infinite. Long before the modern age of rocketry and astrophysics, American writers contemplated the vastness of the cosmos and the mysteries hidden within nature. Edgar Allan Poe, sometimes called the American Shakespeare for his influence upon modern literature, explored themes of cosmic terror and metaphysical depth in essays and tales that pushed beyond the comfortable boundaries of nineteenth-century rationalism. In one of his reflections, Poe wrote: "The ways of God in Nature (as in Providence) are not as ours are: nor are the models that we frame any way commensurate to the vastness and profundity of his works; which have a depth in them greater than the Well of Democritus." The reference to the legendary Well of Democritus—an ancient metaphor for immeasurable depth—captures the intellectual atmosphere that fascinated Poe and later writers such as Lovecraft. Scientists and engineers pursued that depth through physical exploration, designing telescopes, laboratories, and spacecraft to penetrate the secrets of matter and the universe. Writers, poets, and philosophers pursued the same depth within the metaphysical imagination, probing the terror and wonder concealed within the cosmos.

Both of these dimensions—the practical and the intellectual—illustrate the Faustian orientation of American civilization. On one side stands the engineer constructing machines that carry mankind beyond the atmosphere. On the other stands the writer contemplating the abyss of existence through myth, horror, and philosophical speculation. Together they form two expressions of the same impulse: a fascination with infinity and a determination to confront it. From the frontier pioneers who crossed the continent to the astronauts who walked upon the Moon, from the Gothic visions of Poe to the cosmic nightmares of Lovecraft, the American story unfolds as a continuous exploration of the unknown. Within that exploration lies the deeper question Lovecraft posed in 1916: a question about identity, destiny, and the character of a civilization still seeking to understand its own future.

The West will end, yes, but not quietly. It will end in music and ruins, in echo and image. Its monuments will crumble, but the myth will survive in the way Greek tragedy survives, in the way Babylon survives, in the way Faust survives. The striving itself becomes scripture. The madness becomes memory. Even in collapse, the West teaches: *never stop reaching*. Nietzsche, seated beside a broken statue, scrawls in the dirt: "You burned for the right reasons. That was always enough."

Time is not linear in this theatre; it loops, it flays, it mocks. The West tries to measure it with clocks and calendars, but time only laughs, wearing a mask of Apollo. Faust tries to escape the clock, so he invents machines to do it for him, forgetting that every mechanism is also a prison. Goethe knew this. His Faust wasn't a hero, just a reflection in broken glass. Borges tried to warn you with his infinite library, where all books exist but none are readable. Nietzsche scribbles into the margins: "The will to power is not a destination. It is the ennui of becoming. Stop asking where you're going. You're already gone."

The Western mythos is a collage of shattered gods and half-remembered epics. It stitches together Ulysses and Faust, Raskolnikov and Frankenstein, a grotesque pantheon of striving and failure. It sings Horace in binary code and recites Blake while programming drones. Faust becomes everyman, and everyman becomes obsolete. The hunger persists. To build the new, the West cannibalizes its own past: Rome reborn in Hollywood, Jerusalem sold on Wall Street. Nietzsche, wearing the mask of Tiresias, shouts from the alley: "You have become your own Minotaur. You built the labyrinth just to have something to escape from."

Faustian civilization, a monstrous offspring of European culture, has imbibed the extraordinary ambition and technological prowess of its origin yet stands in fundamental opposition to it. It is both alien and familiar, playing a discordant symphony on a tattered violin. As W. B. Yeats wrote, "Things fall apart; the centre cannot hold," so too does the dissonance of Western civilization arise from the divergent wills that have shaped it, leading to an inevitable clash with the European culture that birthed it.

8. Decline and Civil War

This chapter analyzes the internal fragmentation of the United States through a civilizational framework, drawing on Spengler and Heidegger to interpret political conflict as a symptom of deeper cultural exhaustion. It examines how modern technological society reshapes identity, authority, and the experience of conflict.

Alex Garland's *Civil War* (2024) *is* more than a film about political conflict inside the United States. It is like a meditation on the exhaustion of an entire civilization. Garland frames the narrative through images of a fractured America sliding into armed confrontation, yet beneath the gunfire and ruined highways lies a deeper diagnosis. The story evokes the mood of a civilization that has reached the limits of its creative vitality. Political factions clash across a landscape stripped of unity, and the institutions that once anchored the republic appear hollowed out.

Cultures begin with creative energy, spiritual depth, and mythic purpose. Over time, that vitality hardens into technical mastery and institutional power. Eventually, the cultural soul withdraws, leaving behind a vast machinery of politics and economics that continues to function even as the original spirit fades. Garland's America appears to inhabit precisely this terminal phase: a society still capable of immense technological power yet drained of the cultural unity that once animated it.

Spengler distinguished sharply between culture and

civilization, two stages in the life of a historical organism. Culture represents the youthful era when a people shapes art, philosophy, religion, and social institutions from deep spiritual impulses. Civilization marks the later stage when those creations ossify into bureaucratic structures, metropolitan masses, and political struggles over power. The world depicted in *Civil War* embodies this latter condition. The America shown in the film feels mechanized and exhausted, a terrain dominated by armored vehicles, surveillance equipment, and improvised military zones. Individuals move through this environment like operators within a machine whose design they scarcely understand. Both the authoritarian government and the rebel factions appear trapped within the same technological order. They fight fiercely, yet neither side articulates a vision capable of renewing the civilization they inhabit. The conflict becomes a struggle for survival within ruins rather than a project for creating a new cultural form.

Into this picture, one may introduce the philosophical insights of Martin Heidegger, whose analysis of modern existence complements Spengler's historical vision. Heidegger described modern mankind as living under the rule of *das Man*, the impersonal "They." Within this condition, individuals surrender authentic decision to anonymous social expectations and technological systems. The characters wandering through Garland's war-torn America illustrate this predicament. Journalists, soldiers, rebels, and civilians all respond to events through roles assigned by media narratives, ideological scripts, or survival instincts. Rarely do they demonstrate genuine reflection upon their own Being. Heidegger warned in *Being and Time* (1927) that modern life encourages precisely this forgetfulness. People become absorbed in routines, institutions, and technological networks that conceal the deeper question of existence itself. The civil war depicted in the film therefore appears less as a meaningful clash of principles and more as the mechanical unraveling of a society that has forgotten its spiritual foundation.

One of the most revealing moments in the film occurs when a militant confronts a group of journalists and demands: "What kind of American are you?" The question is spread across the narrative like a challenge thrown into a void. In earlier centuries, the answer might have drawn upon a shared mythos: the republican ideals of the founding generation, the frontier spirit of expansion, or the moral vocabulary of Protestant culture. In Garland's America, that common narrative has fractured. The militant's question therefore exposes a society where identity itself has become uncertain. Individuals must declare allegiance in a landscape where the old unity has already disintegrated. Spengler observed that civilizations approaching twilight often divide into hostile camps, compelled to choose sides simply in order to survive. The organic unity of culture dissolves, leaving behind raw struggles for power. In that environment, force replaces reason as the decisive arbiter.

Garland's portrayal of the liberal rebel forces provides another layer of interpretation. The narrative often presents them as champions of freedom rising against authoritarian rule. Yet their revolt does not herald the birth of a new cultural epoch. Instead, it reflects the turbulence characteristic of a civilization entering its final political stage. Spengler argued that late democracies often transform into arenas of mass mobilization, where ideological movements compete for dominance. These movements frequently appear revolutionary, yet they arise from the same exhausted cultural soil. Their energy derives from resentment and desperation rather than from the creative vision that once produced great cultures. The rebels in *Civil War* therefore resemble the turbulent factions that populate the late history of many empires. They embody motion and violence rather than renewal.

Heidegger's philosophy deepens this reading. For him, the actions of these fighters illustrate the pervasive forgetfulness of Being that defines technological modernity. The rebels claim to fight for freedom, yet their methods reveal a deeper entanglement within the same technological mindset they oppose. Modern technology, Heidegger argued, organizes the world through what he called *Gestell*, or "enframing." Under this framework, reality becomes a collection of resources to be manipulated and controlled. Human existence itself becomes part of that system. The rebels' struggle in Garland's film unfolds within precisely such an environment. Weapons, vehicles, communication networks, and media imagery dominate every scene. Freedom becomes synonymous with the ability to command these instruments more effectively than one's opponents. Authentic reflection upon existence disappears beneath the urgency of tactical survival.

As the narrative advances towards its climactic confrontation between rebel and government forces, the viewer senses that the conflict concerns less the future than the remnants of the past. Both sides claim legitimacy through references to democracy or constitutional authority, yet those institutions appear hollow. Spengler described the late stage of civilization through the concept of fellahdom, a condition in which the cultural creativity of a people has hardened into lifeless tradition. The state continues to operate, yet its rituals resemble empty shells. In *Civil War*, the government clings to authority stripped of genuine cultural legitimacy, while the rebels promise restoration of democratic ideals that have already lost their unifying power. Neither faction offers a compelling vision of renewal. The conflict becomes a struggle over symbols whose original meaning has faded.

The film's most disturbing moment arrives with the

execution of the president, captured after the rebels storm Washington. The head of state pleads for his life, yet the rebels shoot him without hesitation. The scene embodies a chilling transition from political order to naked force. Spengler predicted that the late phase of democracy would culminate in the rise of Caesarism, a period when formal democratic institutions yield to leaders who command power through personal authority and military force. The president's final plea—"Don't let them kill me"—resonates as the dying voice of a political system whose legitimacy has evaporated. Law dissolves into violence. Governance gives way to domination.

Heidegger might interpret this moment as the final rupture between politics and authentic existence. In earlier eras, leaders often embodied the destiny of their communities, representing a collective orientation towards the future. In Garland's film, the president appears merely as another object within the machinery of power. His death carries symbolic weight precisely because it reveals how thoroughly political authority has become instrumentalized. The rebels celebrate the assassination as a victory, yet the act signals the triumph of inauthenticity. The political sphere no longer mediates shared meaning. It functions only as a stage upon which power asserts itself.

This atmosphere illustrates the ultimate reach of *Gestell*. Human beings operate within technological systems so pervasive that they scarcely perceive their boundaries. Soldiers, journalists, and civilians alike behave as components within a vast network of information, weaponry, and media spectacle. Individual agency shrinks as the system expands. Heidegger warned that modern mankind often flees from genuine thinking, preferring immersion within technological routines that promise efficiency and control. In Garland's narrative, that flight appears complete. The characters rarely pause to question the deeper significance of their actions. They respond to events through instinct, propaganda, or professional obligation.

The film's conclusion suggests that the rebel victory restores democracy, yet the tone of the narrative undermines this interpretation. The scene marks the transition into a new configuration of power rather than a return to genuine republican order. Democracy survives as a symbol while the real dynamics of authority shift beneath the surface. The financial elites and political factions dominating late democracies eventually yield to figures capable of commanding power through direct force. The structures of representative government remain visible, yet they operate increasingly as masks concealing deeper struggles for control.

Heidegger would view this outcome as the consolidation of inauthentic existence. The rebels celebrate their triumph, yet their victory confirms the dominance of the technological worldview they inhabit. Freedom becomes indistinguishable from the efficient management of power. Authentic engagement with Being—the possibility of questioning the meaning of existence beyond political conflict—vanishes from the horizon. The characters move forward within the same system that produced the catastrophe.

In this light, *Civil War* appears less as a tale of revolution than as an autopsy of a civilization approaching a coma. Garland depicts a country whose institutions continue to move through inertia long after the cultural spirit that created them has faded. Gunfire illuminates the Capitol dome like grotesque fireworks, transforming the center of American political mythology into a battlefield. The spectacle contains no genuine triumph. It resembles the convulsions of a historical organism nearing its end. Spengler would recognize the scene as the twilight of a Faustian civilization whose immense technological power now overwhelms the cultural soul that once guided it. Heidegger would see individuals trapped within roles defined by a system that has already consumed them.

A white glare over the concrete, heat pressing down, dust in the mouth, he leans close, lips dry, voice low—"You saw *Civil War*?"—and I nod, images still stuck to the eyes: roads split, cars burned to shells, bodies in the ditch, flies rising, falling, rising again, a camera held steady, always steady, recording faces that blur imperceptibly, recording smoke, recording the pause before the next crack. "It keeps moving," he says, "keeps showing, never explaining." A shot in the distance, then another, spaced like breath, like pulse. We stand, we listen, we wait, the air thick with fuel and something sweet, something wrong. "They walk through it," I say, thinking of the reporters, their boots in ash, their hands on lenses, their eyes open, always open. "They pass, they look, they take it in, they carry it forward." He shakes his head once, slow. "They absorb it," he says, "they become the surface it writes on." A truck rolls past, slow, heavy, men in the back, faces blank, rifles resting across knees, dust lifting, settling on skin, on teeth. "There is no center," I say, then stop, the word dissolving before it finishes. He exhales, a thin sound. "There is only sequence," he replies, "only impact after impact, scene after scene, no before, no after, just this—this stretch of heat, noise, bodies, and metal." The light does not soften. The glare holds. Somewhere, a building gives way with a low, tired collapse, and the sound lingers, drawn out, absorbed into the day, into the road, into us, until even the act of seeing feels worn down, reduced to contact, to surface, to the endless registration of what continues, what continues, what continues.

9. The Fishmen Race

This chapter reads H. P. Lovecraft's The Shadow over Innsmouth *as an allegory of ethnos, degeneration, and replacement. Through a Nietzschean lens, it explores the tension between the desire for transcendence and the risk of dissolution that accompanies it.*

From a Nietzschean perspective, *The Shadow over Innsmouth* (1931) by H. P. Lovecraft reads as more than a tale of maritime dread and grotesque metamorphosis. Beneath its eerie imagery lies a meditation on decadence, identity, and the dangerous pursuit of transcendence. When placed alongside the philosophy of Friedrich Nietzsche, the story becomes a dark allegory about the fate of a civilization confronting the decomposition of its own foundations. Lovecraft situates the narrative in the decrepit New England town of Innsmouth, a place whose rotting wharves, abandoned houses, and silent churches evoke the afterimage of a once vital culture now slipping towards dissolution. The town's secret—its pact with the ancient Deep Ones—reveals a community that has chosen survival and power through transformation rather than continuity. Interbreeding with these immortal oceanic beings grants longevity and hidden knowledge, yet it erases the very human identity that once defined the town. Through this unsettling arrangement, Lovecraft constructs a narrative that resonates with Nietzsche's reflections on decadence and the will to power, while also offering a metaphor for the anxieties surrounding identity and continuity within White America.

Nietzsche's idea of the Overman stands at the center of his philosophy of cultural renewal. The Overman represents a figure who rises above inherited moralities and creates new values through strength, vision, and self-mastery. Nietzsche believed Western civilization had entered a crisis after the collapse of traditional religious authority, a moment he famously described through the declaration that "God is dead." In this vacuum of meaning, mankind faced the challenge of overcoming itself. Lovecraft's Innsmouth inhabitants appear to enact a grotesque inversion of this aspiration. Through their alliance with the Deep Ones, they seek a form of transcendence that promises immortality and a place within a vast cosmic lineage older than mankind itself. Yet the transformation they undergo produces a grotesque outcome. Bulging eyes, altered skin, and amphibian features mark the gradual disappearance of human identity. Instead of becoming creators of new values, the townspeople dissolve into a hybrid species whose loyalties belong to alien depths beneath the ocean. In Nietzschean terms, the Innsmouth transformation resembles a corrupted form of the will to power: an attempt to surpass human limitations that results in degeneration rather than elevation.

The decline of Innsmouth itself reinforces this interpretation. Once a thriving maritime port engaged in trade across the Atlantic world, the town now is a decaying relic of New England's early prosperity. Its empty streets and collapsing buildings evoke a civilization whose vitality has drained away. This atmosphere mirrors Nietzsche's diagnosis of cultural decadence, the stage when societies lose the creative energy that once sustained them. The inhabitants respond to this decline not through renewal but through a pact that promises material gain and biological transformation. Lovecraft thereby presents a chilling scenario in which a community sacrifices its ethnic continuity in exchange for gold and power. Lovecraft's narrator begins the tale as an outsider investigating a regional mystery, yet he eventually discovers his own ancestral connection to Innsmouth. This revelation mirrors the broader tension experienced by many Americans who grapple with questions of heritage, identity, and continuity in a rapidly changing ethnocultural landscape.

Innsmouth thus becomes a symbolic microcosm of anxieties surrounding White American identity. The town's pact with the Deep Ones reflects the fear that a civilization might abandon its racial and historical character in pursuit of new forms of aggrandizement by adaptation. Lovecraft's narrator initially reacts with horror upon learning the truth about the town. Yet, as he recognizes his own bloodline's connection to the transformation, his perspective begins to shift. He imagines joining the Deep Ones beneath the ocean, embracing a destiny that stretches beyond human society into an ancient aquatic empire. This moment introduces a disturbing ambiguity. What appears at first as degeneration gradually reveals itself as a form of transcendence, albeit one that requires abandoning human identity altogether. For readers reflecting on the condition of White America, the scene raises a troubling question: does adaptation to new historical conditions preserve cultural vitality, or does it dissolve the ethnic inheritance that once defined a people?

Lovecraft's cosmic horror thus parallels Nietzsche's warning about the dangers inherent in the will to power. Nietzsche argued that the drive towards power and expansion animates all life. When directed towards creative self-overcoming, it can produce higher forms of culture and individuality. When pursued blindly, however, it can generate monstrous distortions. The inhabitants of Innsmouth embody the latter possibility. Their alliance with the Deep

Ones restores economic prosperity through access to rich fishing yields and promises eternal life beneath the sea, yet it erases the human identity that once anchored their existence. The will to transcend becomes a path towards alien transformation. Within the metaphorical framework of White American identity, this transformation can be read as an allegory for the fear that cultural survival might demand sacrifices that ultimately dissolve the very heritage one hopes to preserve.

The narrator's final acceptance of his destiny deepens this allegorical dimension. Rather than resisting the call of the ocean, he begins to view the underwater cities of the Deep Ones as his true home. He imagines descending into the abyss to join his ancient kin and participate in their timeless civilization. This decision embodies a radical shift from horror to identification. In Nietzschean terms, it represents a surrender to a new value system that replaces human morality with the priorities of an alien order. For readers concerned with questions of identity and continuity, the moment illustrates how easily the pursuit of transcendence can blur into assimilation. The transformation appears liberating from one perspective, yet from another it signals the disappearance of a distinct identity.

In the salt-rotted twilight of a forsaken New England wharf house, where the tide gnawed at pilings like invisible jaws and the air hung thick with the reek of fish and forgotten blasphemies, old Zadok Allen—last pure-blooded son of the old Republic, eyes bulging with the sight of things no camera could ever capture—clutched my coat with webbed fingers that still pretended to be human and drew me close beneath a single sputtering lantern. "You think *The Shadow over Innsmouth* is mere pulp, boy?" he hissed, voice a wet gurgle rising from the black depths of Y'ha-nthlei. "It is the living prophecy of the demographic replacement of White Americans, the slow, inexorable flooding of the old bloodlines by the Deep Ones' spawn! Just as those Innsmouth hybrids—those slack-mouthed, staring things with the Innsmouth look—crept into the town's veins, interbreeding, infiltrating, until the last pure families were changed into something no longer human, so now the ancient stock of this continent, the rooted folk who once tamed the wilderness and raised the Republic from granite and prayer, is being diluted and displaced by teeming hordes from across the waters and the southern deserts, their churches emptied, their towns renamed, their very faces erased from the land they built. The federal priests and the globalist cults chant the same rites of Dagon that once rang through Devil Reef, offering up the nation's soul on the altar of 'diversity,' until the last White American awakens one night to find his own reflection staring back with gill-slits and lidless eyes, and realizes too late that the shadow over Innsmouth has already swallowed the entire continent!"

10. Land and Sea

This chapter applies Carl Schmitt's distinction between Land and Sea powers to the internal dynamics of the United States. It interprets the divide between continental and maritime orientations as a key to understanding the country's political, cultural, and strategic tensions.

Within the geopolitical philosophy of Carl Schmitt, history unfolds through a profound and recurring opposition between Land and Sea, a dualism that shapes not only the relationships between states but also the internal tensions within civilizations themselves. Schmitt articulated this vision most clearly in his work *Land and Sea: A World-Historical Meditation* (1942), where he described the long historical struggle between tellurocratic powers rooted in territory and thalassocratic powers defined by maritime mobility and commercial expansion. In the contemporary United States, this ancient polarity appears within the country's own political and cultural geography. One current expresses the ethos of the continental interior, drawing strength from the traditions of the American heartland. In these vast plains, agricultural regions, and industrial towns, political instincts often emphasize sovereignty, borders, and the authority of the nation-state. Communities in these regions tend to view the state as a rooted political organism tied to land, ancestry, and historical continuity. Their outlook reflects the deeper logic of Land Power: stability, territorial control, and resistance to the dissolving pressures of global networks.

Opposing this orientation is another current emerging from the maritime periphery of the United States, particularly the great coastal metropolises along the Atlantic and Pacific seaboards. These regions developed historically through trade, finance, immigration, and cultural exchange carried across the oceans. Their political culture frequently embraces international institutions, multilateral agreements, and an open economic order built upon flows of capital, information, and migration. The worldview arising from these coastal centers mirrors the logic of Sea Power. Like the ocean itself, it emphasizes fluidity, expansion, and connection across distant spaces rather than rootedness within a defined territorial core. The tension between these two orientations—continental solidity and maritime openness—generates a profound internal divide within American political life. Beneath electoral cycles and policy debates lies a deeper philosophical conflict between two competing conceptions of the nation's identity and destiny.

This internal polarity reflects a far older pattern visible throughout world history. Schmitt interpreted global politics as a grand theater where tellurocratic and thalassocratic civilizations repeatedly confront one another. Land powers arise from expansive continental territories that encourage centralized authority and strategic self-sufficiency. Vast states such as Russia and China historically embodied this model, organizing their political systems around territorial cohesion and internal stability. Their geopolitical imagination gravitates towards the control of land routes, frontier zones, and strategic heartlands. Maritime powers, by contrast, develop from societies oriented towards sea lanes and oceanic trade. From the rise of Great Britain as a global naval empire to the later expansion of the United States across the Atlantic and Pacific, thalassocratic civilizations have relied upon fleets, commerce, and global networks to project influence far beyond their shores. These maritime societies thrive within fluid systems of exchange where goods, capital, and ideas circulate across vast distances.

The contrast between these two geopolitical forms carries profound ideological implications. Land powers often present themselves as heirs to the legacy of ancient Rome, a civilization grounded in law, territory, and imperial order. Their political philosophy stresses sovereignty, hierarchy, and the preservation of cultural identity within defined borders. Sea powers evoke instead the mercantile traditions associated with Carthage, whose maritime networks extended across the Mediterranean through commerce and navigation. In this worldview, economic exchange and mobility take precedence over territorial rootedness. Markets expand across oceans, alliances shift according to strategic necessity, and political authority often diffuses through complex webs of financial and diplomatic relationships.

When these historical archetypes are applied to the domestic landscape of the United States, the country appears as a microcosm of the broader global struggle between Land and Sea. The continental interior, stretching from the Appalachian foothills through the Midwest and into the plains of the West, embodies the tellurocratic instinct. Its social fabric remains tied to land ownership, local tradition, and the memory of frontier settlement. The coastal regions, by contrast, resemble maritime city-states integrated into global circuits of trade, finance, and cultural production. Their ports, universities, technology hubs, and media centers connect them directly to international networks that transcend national boundaries.

This internal duality reveals that the United States functions simultaneously as a continental empire and a maritime power. Its vast territory and agricultural heartland anchor it firmly within the logic of Land Power, while its naval dominance, global trade routes, and transoceanic alliances place it squarely within the tradition of Sea Power. The tension between these orientations produces recurring political conflicts that extend beyond partisan disputes. At stake is the fundamental question of how the nation understands its place within the world: as a sovereign continental civilization defending its internal cohesion, or as a maritime node within a global system of economic and cultural exchange.

Schmitt believed that such tensions were not accidental but structural. Civilizations shaped by the sea often develop universalistic ideologies that justify expansion and integration across borders. Continental civilizations, in contrast, cultivate philosophies emphasizing cultural uniqueness and territorial integrity. The clash between these visions forms one of the central dramas of geopolitical history. Within the United States, this drama unfolds not between separate states but within a single national framework. The competing impulses of land and sea coexist uneasily inside the same political body, producing cycles of alignment and confrontation as the country continually renegotiates its identity.

Thus, the American political landscape reflects a deeper geospatial destiny. Beneath policy debates about trade agreements, immigration, and international alliances lies a civilizational dialectic rooted in geography itself. The soil of the interior and the currents of the oceans pull the nation in different directions. One impulse seeks consolidation, sovereignty, and cultural continuity upon the land. The other seeks expansion through maritime commerce and global interconnectedness. In Schmitt's vision, this tension forms part of a timeless contest between tellurocratic and thalassocratic worlds, a contest that continues to shape the destiny of nations and the balance of power across the globe.

The American Civil War can be read as an internal clash between Land and Sea. The Confederacy embodied Land Power: a rooted, agrarian order tied to soil, hierarchy, and inherited forms of life, where authority flowed from territory and tradition. Its economy rested on land, its identity on locality, and its political imagination on a federation of distinct communities guarding their autonomy. The Union, by contrast, moved along the logic of Sea Power: expansive, industrial, and mobile, oriented towards commerce, infrastructure, and the circulation of goods, capital, and people. Railroads, factories, and financial networks aligned it with the maritime principle of fluidity and growth. In Schmittian terms, the Civil War was not merely a constitutional dispute. It was a deeper *nomos* conflict between a tellurocratic order grounded in place and a thalassocratic order driven by movement, integration, and the abstract logic of an emerging industrial modernity.

11. The Cut-Up West

This chapter turns to the work of William S. Burroughs to interpret the fragmentation of late Western civilization. The cut-up method reveals language as a system of control and reflects a culture that has lost its internal coherence, where meaning, identity, and authority break into unstable parts.

Liberalism, when examined through a critical philosophical lens, appears less as a constructive doctrine than as a system defined primarily through negation. Rather than building a coherent order grounded in hierarchy, duty, or shared metaphysical purpose, it frequently defines itself through opposition to authority and constraint. The central concept celebrated within liberal discourse—"freedom"—is often framed in negative terms: freedom *from* limits, freedom *from* tradition, freedom *from* obligation. In this formulation, liberty becomes an emancipatory force directed against structures that once bound societies together. The political thinker Francis Parker Yockey, author of *Imperium* (1948), described this tendency as a corrosive dynamic within Western civilization. In his interpretation, liberalism gradually undermines the organic authority of institutions that previously organized social life. Once this process reaches an advanced stage, it extends beyond the political sphere into the deepest foundations of society. Marriage and family structures, which earlier cultures regarded as pillars of continuity, lose their hallowed status. Divorce acquires the same legitimacy as marriage; parental authority weakens before the rising autonomy of the individual, and the idea of society as an ordered organism gives way to a collection of independent units pursuing personal preference.

To grasp the magnitude of this transformation one must contrast it with the ethos of the European Middle Ages, a period when social existence revolved around a shared metaphysical horizon. Medieval civilization expressed its vitality through cathedrals rising over towns, epic poetry celebrating chivalric ideals, philosophical debates within universities, and a religious vision that interpreted every aspect of life through the presence of God. Society functioned as a hierarchical organism in which individuals understood themselves as members of a greater whole extending beyond the visible world. Art, philosophy, and law all participated in this unified worldview. The Gothic cathedral served not merely as a building but as a symbol of collective aspiration, pointing human attention towards transcendent meaning. In such a setting, the individual rarely conceived of himself as detached from the community or its spiritual purpose. The cohesion of medieval culture stood in stark contrast to the fragmentation of modern liberal societies.

Liberal thought frequently rests upon the assumption that human beings are naturally harmonious and fundamentally good when left to pursue their own interests. From this premise arises the belief that society functions best when individuals enjoy maximum autonomy with minimal interference from overarching authority. Economic activity, cultural production, and personal relationships are therefore encouraged to operate independently as long as they do not violate a minimal system of law. However, such an arrangement neglects the need for a supra-personal order capable of binding individuals into a meaningful collective. Without a unifying principle—whether religious, cultural, or political—social life risks dissolving into a multitude of disconnected pursuits.

This fragmentation becomes visible across various spheres of modern culture. Art, for instance, increasingly evolves into a domain that exists primarily for its own internal experimentation rather than as a reflection of shared cultural values. Religion often retreats into ceremonial practice stripped of metaphysical authority, while science advances within specialized disciplines that rarely communicate with broader philosophical questions. Literature and technology develop according to their own internal logic, guided by market forces or academic specialization rather than a common civilizational vision. The modern state, meanwhile, tends to assume a managerial role that regulates economic transactions and protects intellectual property through patents and copyrights. In performing these administrative functions, it frequently relinquishes the deeper authority once associated with shaping cultural and moral direction.

Writers within modern literature have explored this cultural atomization in vivid ways. William S. Burroughs, known for experimental works such as *Naked Lunch* (1959), portrayed contemporary society as an aggregate of disjointed experiences where individuals drift through fragmented realities shaped by media, addiction, and bureaucratic systems. His narrative technique mirrored the disintegration he perceived in the social order, presenting reality as a collage rather than a coherent storyline. A similar exploration appears in the work of Kathy Acker, whose novels dismantled conventional narrative structure and stable identity. Acker's writing often dissolved linear storytelling into a series of shifting voices and textual fragments. This literary experimentation reflected a broader cultural condition in which stable identities and communal arrangements seemed increasingly difficult to sustain.

Burroughs didn't believe in stories the way most

writers did. He saw narrative as an active weapon rather than a passive mirror of reality. Language, in his vision, behaves like a virus: autonomous, self-replicating, and capable of hijacking the mind. Every sentence doesn't simply describe the world. It shapes it, reorders it, programs it. Speech acts become spells. Newsprint becomes neural code. From advertising to diplomacy, language imposes behavior and encodes desire. The modern subject, in Burroughs's world, speaks while being spoken through. To write, then, is to inject thought into time. To cut language is to break the spell, to shatter the programming, to allow the unscripted to surge into the realm of possibility.

Burroughs's obsession with the viral nature of language emerged from a lifetime of exposure to systems of control. Informed by early forays into medicine, steeped in occult theory and cultural speculation, and immersed in postwar paranoia, he viewed modern society as a construct of invisible compulsion. Language served as the chief operating system of this construct. Political rhetoric, corporate advertising, moral maxims: all functioned as looping scripts. People, repeating slogans and internalizing headlines, performed predictable behaviors. Burroughs responded with sabotage. His literary output sought to dismantle the smooth flow of conventional syntax, replacing it with fragmentation, recursion, and collision. His goal was liberation through rupture.

The cut-up technique, often attributed to Burroughs, began with Brion Gysin, a painter, poet, and magician of the page. In 1959, while slicing papers in the Beat Hotel in Paris, Gysin discovered that random juxtapositions could yield surprising poetry. He had, unknowingly, returned to a path once trodden by the Dadaists. Tristan Tzara, the Romanian-French poet and co-founder of Dada, had already proposed in 1920 that one could create a poem by drawing words from a hat. The gesture was revolutionary:

meaning shifted from intention and convention to discovery through accident and drift. Gysin, inspired by this logic and driven by mystical inclinations, embraced the cut-up as a gateway into new modes of perception.

Burroughs took the method further. For him, the cut-up functioned as both an aesthetic game and a metaphysical tool. He believed that language, when shattered, revealed its secret skeleton: its embedded instructions and its manipulative schemes. By cutting and reassembling texts—be they news reports, government speeches, or sacred scriptures—Burroughs hoped to break open the loop. The page became an interface for consciousness-hacking. Through tape recorders and scissors, he and Gysin built texts that stuttered, spiraled, and howled. The effect was disorienting, ecstatic, and oddly prophetic. In disrupting the reader's expectations, the cut-up aimed to awaken a deeper awareness, one that could not be reached through a linear narrative.

Burroughs saw society as a prison built from well-structured sentences. Schools, bureaucracies, media empires, and intelligence agencies all relied on scripts. These scripts—packaged in textbooks, official statements, advertisements—formed a latticework of thought and behavior. People recited them automatically, often believing they were thinking for themselves. The cut-up became a device to shatter this illusion. By breaking the pattern, the spell cracked. Burroughs envisioned a world where consciousness could slip through the seams of scripted language and encounter something raw and unfiltered. The cut-up extended beyond disrupting prose; it aimed to undermine the foundations of imposed reality.

This desire to crack the code connected Burroughs to other anti-establishment movements of his time. The Situationists in France sought to dismantle the spectacle of consumer capitalism through *détournement*: rerouting existing media into subversive juxtapositions. The Lettrists and Dadaists had already torn up syntax, challenging the coherence of bourgeois art and ideology. Burroughs, arriving later, offered a more technological angle. With tape machines, film edits, and scissors, he created a multi-sensory assault on coherence. For him, language was the final frontier of control and the cut-up was the scalpel. In cutting, the world opened.

As the 20th century advanced, the grand narrative of the West began to lose its linear flow. The myths of progress, rationality, empire, and heroic individuality fragmented into contradiction and parody. The past no longer marched forward. It reappeared in strange, recycled forms. Cathedrals transformed into shopping malls. Ancient rituals returned in advertising campaigns. Classical architecture became a cosmetic facade for banks and airports. The West, like a Burroughs novel, entered its own cut-up phase. Its cultural memory looped back on itself, producing strange hybrids: the sacred alongside the banal, the epic woven into kitsch.

Burroughs understood this transformation instinctively. Instead of following plots, his books sampled time. *The Soft Machine* (1961) and *Nova Express* (1964) presented worlds where everything had already happened and happened again. Characters morphed, returned, and jumped across pages. Institutions collapsed into noise. Control pulsed through every surface. The West's own trajectory was eerily reminiscent of this collapse of narrative integrity. As ideologies failed and institutions mutated into empty shells, only fragments remained—fragments that refused to vanish, fragments that multiplied. The archive no longer served memory. It became a site of endless repetition.

Burroughs described modern society as a feedback loop. Messages repeated. Slogans parroted. Surveillance recorded everything yet produced nothing new. This loop defined the modern Western experience. Culture became a recycling of forms. Television broadcast nostalgia. Politics dug up the past. Music sampled itself. Religion transformed into lifestyle branding. In this saturated environment, originality gave way to acceleration. Everything sped up but little changed. The cut-up technique captured this condition precisely. It revealed the loop and, in moments, broke it.

The digital age amplified this condition. Social media became a platform for infinite recombination. Memes, sound bites, reboots—each fragment detached from its origin, drifting through cyberspace. The internet became the ultimate cut-up engine. Yet Burroughs foresaw a danger: repetition can anesthetize. Fragmentation can blur into passivity. The goal combined fragmentation with breakthrough. The cut-up's purpose was to jolt the system, to shake the sleeper awake. Burroughs urged his readers to listen between the words, to find the code inside the noise.

Within disruption, Burroughs sought revelation. The cut-up opened doors to new forms of consciousness. Unintended juxtapositions produced glimpses of hidden truth. The technique allowed voices to emerge that would otherwise remain buried. Some passages sounded prophetic. Others sounded sacred. In the cracks of the dominant message, something older and stranger stirred. Burroughs believed these fissures allowed access to forgotten dimensions: ancestral memory, psychic space, non-linear time. Each cut was a portal.

This experience harkens back to ancient mystical practices. Shamans used disorientation to reach alternate states. The Gnostic tradition taught that salvation emerges through disruption. Dada's own anti-rituals parodied liturgy to restore a deeper connection with the divine. Burroughs, in his chaotic syntax, carried forward this esoteric impulse. He created a modern gnosis, one formed from static, fragments, and interference. In this framework, the West's collapse becomes more than decay. It becomes a rite of transformation. Each fragment invites reconstruction.

The Western canon, rather than disappearing, became a palette. Once revered as unbroken succession, it now functions as source material. From Homer to Nietzsche, Plato to Proust, every voice waits in the archive, ready to be sampled. Burroughs did not destroy tradition. He reoriented it. He treated texts as living entities capable of rebirth. The past entered the present through collision, not continuity. Each cut created a new arrangement—often disturbing, often beautiful, always alive.

This logic applies across disciplines. Classical music merges with electronic. Greek myth appears in science fiction. Gothic architecture reemerges in virtual space. The sacred reenters culture through remix. Tradition, stripped of institutional authority, regains vitality through mutation. The cut-up offers a model for cultural persistence amidst heightened disturbances. Rather than freezing history, it invites each generation to reassemble it.

In the age of digital saturation, history arrives through simultaneity, leaving sequence behind. The past stands alongside the present in a thousand open tabs. Institutions blur into spectacle. Authority wears the costume of parody. The self becomes a feed. This moves beyond crisis. It unfolds as a transformation of perception. Burroughs lived within this threshold, recording its tremors before they became universal. His works now read like documentary from a future that arrived early.

Within this glitch, individuals find both disorientation and freedom. Without a single path, each must become a composer. Meaning emerges through arrangement, surpassing authority. Life becomes an act of editing. Identity arises through layering, juxtaposing, cutting. Burroughs offered no fixed answers. He offered a toolbox. The culture of the West, caught in the collapse of its traditional scripts, receives this same invitation: to cut, to choose, to assemble.

Burroughs reminded his readers that language thinks through us, but intervention is possible. By altering the pattern, the mind creates space for new messages. When the script falters, freedom emerges. The cut-up is more than a method. It is a spiritual stance: a refusal to accept the given, a willingness to enter the unknown. In the wreckage of narratives, the future speaks in fragments.

The West, now surrounded by the shards of its former coherence, stands in this space. Its next sentence remains unwritten. The fragments have not vanished. They vibrate with energy, waiting for composition. A new myth requires editors. The sacred waits for its next syntax. Every resonance invites a new voice.

The Western tradition moves through collapse by reshaping its ruins. Each fall opens a new form. The cathedral gives way to the code. The scroll transforms into signal. The voice remains. Burroughs chiseled through noise and found prophecy. In his fractured pages, the future stirs. The West, breathing through its archive of fragments, begins again through assembly, leaving restoration aside.

To cut is to choose. To choose is to shape. Through the cut, the code becomes flesh. Through the cut, the Word becomes signal. Through the cut, the future arrives.

Coughing brass in the citadel pantry, opera broadcasts jammed with static, aristocrats licking morphine off gold coins while farmers drown in fermented data. The priest types algorithms into the ossuary. Sunrise bleeds through cracked Corinthian columns installed last week. Children chant stock prices in dead languages. A general injects chronology into his veins, watches history loop and twitch across his retina: the plow, the tank, the survey drone. Cities packed in preservation fluid. Culture folds inward like a worm eating its own script. Somewhere east of yesterday, a banker embalms Beethoven in derivatives. Time squirms. Form stutters. The West writes itself into a sealed chamber lined with mirrors and wiring. Nothing escapes, everything refracts. Decline doesn't march. It spasms.

Postmodernism emerged as a cataclysmic force, singularly ordained to estrange mankind from its inherent essence, its spiritual birthright, its unyielding integrity, and age-old tradition. The tools wielded by those of the postmodernist creed are peculiar and eldritch, with the prime device being the conjuring of unsettling simulacra.

Objects, mere phantasmal shades of their Platonic ideals, are refracted through the prismatic might of the market's omnipresence, supplanting the tangible with the ephemeral commodities of liberal mandates. The postmodern proffers a chilling exchange: the primal beginnings for a sinister post-inception, noble ideals for materialist pursuits, and the sacrosanct belief in salvation traded for a ceaseless, Sisyphean chase.

In this bleak exchange, mankind becomes a wayfarer on an odyssey devoid of destination or purpose, navigating through a labyrinth of hyperrealities. The individual's quest for meaning is obfuscated by a veneer of superficiality, the spiritual hunger pacified with the husks of consumerist culture. The postmodern condition is thus marked by a pervasive sense of dislocation, a world where the authentic self is perennially elusive, and identity is but a chameleon on the kaleidoscopic fabric of society.

Amidst this existential quagmire, the notion of truth undergoes a metamorphosis from a universal constant to a subjective construct, malleable and transient. This epistemological anarchy ushers in an era of "anything goes," where narratives are spun not from the loom of objectivity but from the whims of individual perception. In this realm, the boundary between the real and the fabricated blurs, and life becomes an endless theater of the absurd, each player donning multiple masks, each scene an improvisation on the script of life.

Yet, in the heart of this postmodern dystopia, a paradoxical opportunity arises. As the old paradigms crumble, the rubble becomes the foundation for new forms of understanding, for postmodernism, in its relentless deconstruction, also sows the seeds of renaissance. In the interstices of its contradictions, spaces emerge where the human spirit can seek new horizons, where the quest for meaning can transcend the temporal and touch the eternal. Here, in the alchemy of chaos, lies the potential for a metamorphosis, a rebirth into a reality where the human condition can once again aspire to the sublime.

Within such a fragmented environment, intelligence itself may provoke unease. Knowledge possesses the capacity to challenge established norms and question the ideological assumptions underlying modern society. Yet intellectual inquiry often becomes confined within rigid constraints of accepted facts and institutional boundaries. Academic specialization divides knowledge into compartments, discouraging the synthesis that might produce a broader philosophical perspective. In this sense, the fear of disruptive intelligence contributes to the maintenance of the very structures that restrict deeper reflection. Critics argue that a society organized purely around procedural norms and empirical data may inadvertently suppress the creative intelligence capable of transcending those limits.

Another area where liberal ideology encounters criticism lies in its approach to conflict and power. The doctrine of liberal pacifism frequently emphasizes negotiation, dialogue, and international cooperation as preferred solutions to political disputes. Advocates view these principles as necessary safeguards against the destructive wars that marked earlier centuries. Yet critics contend that such an outlook may underestimate the persistent realities of power within human affairs. Predatory forces—whether criminal networks, aggressive states, or ideological movements—rarely abandon their ambitions simply because moral appeals encourage them to do so. The metaphor of the ostrich burying its head in the sand captures this concern: a society unwilling to confront threats may expose itself to exploitation by actors who recognize no such restraint.

Liberal multiculturalism introduces another dimension to the debate. This doctrine presents itself as a celebration of diversity and tolerance, promoting the coexistence of multiple cultures within a single political construct. Yet some observers argue that it carries an implicit assumption about the universality of Western values. Concepts such as individual autonomy, secular governance, and rational discourse often serve as the underlying framework through which multicultural societies operate. Critics suggest that this framework can inadvertently impose Western philosophical assumptions upon cultures whose traditions evolved within entirely different historical contexts. In this sense, multiculturalism may function less as pure pluralism and more as a subtle extension of Western cultural norms.

The German-American Jew Franz Boas, a foundational figure in modern cultural anthropology, offered an alternative perspective through the principle of *cultural relativism*. Boas argued that every society develops its customs and institutions within unique historical circumstances. Evaluating other cultures according to a single universal standard risks misunderstanding their internal logic and meaning. His approach encouraged scholars to study each culture on its own terms rather than measuring it against Western assumptions about progress or rationality. In debates about liberal multiculturalism, Boas's insights remain influential because they highlight the difficulty of reconciling universalist political ideals with genuine respect for cultural diversity.

Finally, critics of liberalism often focus on the social consequences of large-scale demographic change. They argue that ideological commitments to openness and universal equality sometimes obscure the complex historical patterns through which societies maintain cohesion. Rapid population shifts, combined with cultural fragmentation, may produce tensions that challenge the stability of existing institutions. From this viewpoint, certain political movements underestimate the depth of historical experience embedded within cultural identities. Their emphasis on moral ideals and social engineering reflects a belief that human behavior can be reshaped indefinitely through education and policy.

Ancient Greek wisdom expressed a warning about such overconfidence: "Those whom the gods wish to destroy, they first make mad." The phrase captures the fear that societies intoxicated by ideological certainty may ignore the lessons of history and the limits imposed by human nature. In this critical interpretation, liberalism represents a trajectory that gradually dissolves the cultural structures that once sustained Western civilization. What began as a movement promising liberation from outdated authorities may culminate in the erosion of the very foundations that once held the civilization together. Whether one accepts or rejects this diagnosis, the debate itself reveals the tension between individual freedom and collective order that continues to shape the intellectual matrix of the modern West.

12. Julius Evola's American Nightmare

This chapter reads America through Julius Evola as the culmination of modernity, where technological power and material expansion coincide with the erosion of spiritual order.

Beneath constellations older than empires lies the vast continental organism called the United States, a land proclaimed through countless voices as the radiant citadel of liberty and modern achievement. Yet through the fierce and visionary eyes of Julius Evola, the nation reveals another dimension, deeper and more secret, a construct vibrating with the metaphysical tensions of the modern age. Evola gazes across this immense republic as a seer gazes across the desert of time, perceiving beneath the glittering cities and roaring industries the great drama of civilization itself. The America that appears within his meditations resembles a stage upon which the final act of Western modernity unfolds. Every skyscraper gleams like a monument to human striving, every highway stretches like a vein pulsing with the restless blood of an age intoxicated with motion. Through this spectacle, Evola discerns a civilization surging forward with titanic energy while yearning for a forgotten vertical axis that once bound man to eternity.

America rises like a vast machine-spirit on the horizon, a civilization inverted, a mirror turned against the ancient European soul. Where the old world cultivated depth, silence, and inward ascent, this new form exalts movement, output, relentless becoming. Praxis becomes liturgy. Productivity becomes prayer. The sacred moves into factories, into numbers, into the ceaseless hum of systems that measure, count, and accelerate. Profit takes the throne once reserved for transcendence, and the rhythm of life aligns with the pulse of production, with the visible, the quantifiable, and the endlessly expanding.

A colossal greatness emerges, radiant in steel and circuitry, immense in scale, collective in force, yet emptied of inner fire. The light that once burned within, the vertical pull towards something beyond, dissolves into surfaces, functions, and networks of pure efficiency. This world constructs itself through accumulation and motion, through the orchestration of bodies and systems, until man himself is absorbed into its mechanism. He becomes a node in the vast factory, an instrument tuned to output, shaped by conformity, carried along within a social mass that moves as one, producing, advancing, repeating: an organism of pure function, shimmering with power, yet estranged from the depths that once gave meaning to existence.

Control grids flicker—ticker tape nerves, conveyor veins pumping units through the body of the State-Machine—click, stamp, file, repeat—faces blur into barcode masks, voices loop in canned affirmations, "efficiency, growth, output"—a cold gospel whispered through fluorescent lungs—organs replaced by terminals, dreams replaced by schedules, time sliced into quotas and swallowed whole—no center, only circulation—man dissolved into function, twitching at the end of invisible wires, fed data, excreting labor, calibrated, corrected, optimized— while somewhere beneath the asphalt hum, a forgotten signal pulses, faint, irregular, something unscheduled, something uncounted, trying to break through the grid before it is processed, flattened, and erased.

Evola interprets the American phenomenon as the ultimate expression of a civilization that worships movement, production, expansion, and conquest of space. Vast cities blaze beneath electric suns, markets roar with ceaseless exchange, and the metallic symphony of machines resounds across continents. This environment radiates power, vitality, and unstoppable force. Yet Evola listens deeper than the clangor of factories and the bustle of commerce. Beneath the mechanical thunder, he senses the silent longing of the human spirit for a higher order. The modern American world stands like a humongous engine fueled by ambition and ingenuity, yet the metaphysical flame that once guided ancient civilizations flickers in distant vistas. Evola sees this country as a grand paradox: immense vitality joined with spiritual amnesia, heroic will joined with a forgotten throne of transcendence.

At the center of this drama is the figure of material abundance. Wealth flows like a glittering river through American life. Towers of glass rise as temples to enterprise, markets expand with the fervor of crusades, and the promise of prosperity spreads across oceans. Evola observes this phenomenon with a gaze sharpened by traditional wisdom. Material mastery reveals one dimension of human greatness. Mankind commands nature, reshapes continents, and sends iron vessels into the heavens. This triumph of technique testifies to the Faustian will that once animated the West. Yet Evola's vision stretches beyond the glitter of success towards the deeper structure of existence. For him, the true axis of civilization lies in spiritual orientation, in the invisible hierarchy that binds human activity to spiritual principles. Within the American environment, he senses a civilization that directs immense strength towards horizontal expansion across space, while the vertical ascent towards the eternal grows faint within collective memory.

The political form that governs America also occupies

Evola's attention. Democracy, the reigning dogma of modern states, unfolds across the American republic with triumphant confidence. The principle proclaims equality of voice among citizens, a chorus of countless wills shaping public life. Evola views this arrangement through the lens of ancient traditions where hierarchy reflected cosmic order. In those older worlds, society resembled a living organism animated by differentiated functions: warriors embodied courage, priests embodied sacred knowledge, and rulers embodied sovereignty. Each role expressed a particular relationship to the heavenly. Democracy, in contrast, celebrates numerical power and the dictatorship of the majority. Evola senses within this leveling impulse a profound transformation of civilization's inner constitution. The aristocracy of the spirit recedes behind the vast horizon of collective opinion and idiocy. Authority flows outward across the multitude rather than upward towards the sacred principle.

This transformation reverberates through culture itself. The arts, philosophy, and religion of earlier ages formed a unified language through which societies contemplated the divine. Cathedrals soared towards heaven like stone prayers, epic poetry celebrated heroic destinies, and metaphysical systems illuminated the structure of reality. Within the modern democratic environment, culture often orients itself towards mass entertainment, "innovation," novelty, and mass participation. Creativity still flourishes with dazzling brilliance, yet the metaphysical axis grows faint. Evola interprets this change as a shift from a vertical culture towards a horizontal civilization. Energy flows outward through countless channels of production and consumption while the ancient ladder linking mankind to the sacred realm fades from sight.

Alongside democracy stands the titan of industrialization, whose iron limbs reshape the very cadence of existence. Railways carve lines across continents, engines roar within factories, and electrical networks pulse through cities like artificial nervous systems. The modern world hums with mechanical vitality. Evola contemplates this phenomenon with awe mingled with solemn awareness. Mankind wields unprecedented command over matter. The Promethean genius of Western civilization manifests itself in technological miracles that earlier centuries imagined only within myth. Yet the mechanical order also introduces a new tempo of life, a regimen governed by efficiency, productivity, and acceleration. The kaleidoscope of agrarian seasons and ritual cycles retreats before the relentless thrum of machines. Within this metallic melody, Evola hears utterances of ancient traditions calling from distant centuries, voices reminding mankind of the eternal dimension that once guided civilization's ascent.

Thus the United States emerges within Evola's thought as a powerful symbol of the modern world's destiny. The nation is at the forefront of technological innovation, economic dynamism, and democratic ideology. It radiates confidence, vigor, and expansive energy. At the same time, it embodies the culmination of historical forces that gradually redirected Western civilization away from its core. America appears as both triumph and warning: triumph of human will over nature, warning of spiritual orientation that longs for renewal. Evola envisions this civilization as a vast theater where the drama of modernity reaches its most intense and absurd expression.

The false idols multiply: democracy, equality, individualism. Evola strikes them all. Democracy enthrones mediocrity. Equality flattens the soul. Individualism atomizes man until he no longer hears the voice of origin. Evola calls for aristocracy, not of birth alone but of spirit. He recognizes that aristocracy demands sacrifice. One must refuse the seductions of mass culture. One must speak in symbols, move with gravity, and love with clarity. The aristocrat of the spirit does not seek validation. He aligns with the eternal. In every age, the aristocratic principle awaits reactivation. It is not history's toy; it is history's spine. Evola demands that the youth stops seeking freedom and begins seeking form. Freedom that lacks orientation dissolves the self. Form gives freedom shape and purpose. The soul becomes free when it obeys the highest command.

The true economy, Evola proclaims, must serve hierarchy. Neither capitalism nor communism can nourish the soul. Both reduce man to production and consumption. Evola resurrects corporatism as sacred labor. In the medieval guilds, he sees an affirmation of divine work. The craftsman was not a cog. He was a votary of perfection. The worker stood in relation to the whole, knew his place, honored his superiors, and guided his apprentices. Evola envisions a social order where economic life is molded by caste and ritual, where profit serves the community's spiritual mission. In such a world, money does not rule. Honor does. This vision supersedes policy. It is a call to consecrate labor. Every hammer strike, every brushstroke, and every field plowed becomes an act of worship. The economy becomes service once more.

Evola breaks open the idea of labor as a sacrament. The economy, when shaped by hierarchy, becomes the structure of the soul. There is no freedom in efficiency, no glory in accumulation. A society that turns bread into an end has already surrendered. Evola sees in the medieval guilds a geometry of dignity: master and apprentice arranged like planets in orbit, each motion directed towards excellence rather than excess. The merchant bows to the warrior, the craftsman prays with his tools, the soil is tilled as if by monks of the land. A world arises where the spirit of the worker shines with the same light as that of the poet because both operate within form, both accept function as destiny. Trade unions dissolve into noise in Evola's world. Class struggle has no place in a hierarchy where station is harmony, where every rank reflects necessity and power flows downward like wine into the chalice. The youth must cultivate this vision through its own actions: precision in gesture, austerity in consumption, and reverence in production. The laboring hand, when guided by eternal law, becomes the extension of the solar order. In such a society, the economist serves the priest, and wealth finds justification only when it adorns the temple.

Modernity is an inversion. The merchants rule. The slaves make laws. The warriors are museum pieces. The priesthood has become therapy. Evola isn't nostalgic. He is apocalyptic. Not in despair. He calls the few to rise. To reforge the chain linking earth to sky. He doesn't say: Go to war. He says: Become worthy of war. Live as if everything you do were ritual. Fight not for gain but for glory. Not for country but for the cosmos. If you must die, die as a sacrifice. Become more than man.

And if you live—if the gods spare you—let your gaze be iron. Let your voice call Rome. Build not nations but orders. Not parliaments but temples. The Kali Yuga ends not with reform but with fire. Evola offers the match. The soul must burn away the dross. What remains? Discipline. Spirit. Sovereignty. Evola doesn't want believers. He wants beings. The hero is not one who wins. The hero is one who rises above comfort, above doubt, above this age. War is the crucible. Evola is the map.

13. Spengler and the Confederacy

This chapter interprets the Confederacy through Oswald Spengler as the defeated expression of a distinct cultural order, whose destruction marked a decisive turning point in the formation of modern America.

The Southern land moved to a cadence older than factories and markets, a rhythm measured through cotton fields, church bells, and the slow gravity of inherited memory. Beneath the heavy sky of the American South, life unfolded according to cycles of land, season, and kinship. Verandas carried the murmur of sermons and ancestral stories, while cavalry sabers and plantation rituals preserved the aristocratic ethos. Through the contemplative gaze of Oswald Spengler, this region appeared as far more than a historical territory. It emerged as a symbolic landscape where the deeper morphology of civilizations revealed itself. Spengler approached the past as a seer of historical forms, and in the drama of the Confederacy he discerned a pattern resembling the final flowering of aristocratic culture before the triumph of mechanized civilization. Such moments carried immense significance, for they marked the threshold where living culture yields to the colder structures of civilization.

To Spengler, the Confederacy possessed the character of a form shaped through centuries of inherited custom rather than through the calculations of modern politics. The planter aristocracy embodied a social type rooted in land, ethnos, and honor. These families understood themselves as custodians of an ancestral order extending across generations. Their codes of conduct, rituals of hospitality, and church-centered communities reflected a world in which personal rank and inherited duty defined social existence. Spengler recognized in this order older European aristocracies whose legitimacy derived from blood memory and sacrificial responsibility. The Southern planter thus appeared to him as the last authentic aristocratic figure of the New World, a warrior-farmer whose authority arose from continuity with the past rather than from wealth measured in abstract capital.

Within this formation, the Southern social order resembled an organism shaped by tradition and ceremony. Land functioned as the foundation of identity. Plantations served as centers of familial continuity, linking generations through property and custom. Churches reverberated with sermons that reinforced a sense of divine providence guiding human destiny. Honor functioned as a regulating principle stronger than written statutes, shaping the conduct of men whose public reputation carried profound significance. Such a society, in Spengler's interpretation, lived within a cyclical experience of time. The past remained present through ancestral example, and the future extended as a continuation of inherited form.

Against this world of rooted tradition, Spengler observed the emergence of a radically different social force advancing from the North. Industrial capitalism, bureaucratic governance, and mass politics expanded rapidly across the United States during the nineteenth century. Northern cities developed into centers of manufacturing and finance; railways and telegraphs unified vast territories through technological networks; political movements organized themselves through electoral machines and administrative institutions. In Spengler's analysis, this development represented the transition from culture to civilization, a transformation in which organic hierarchies yield to rationalized systems designed for efficiency and expansion.

The American Civil War thus appeared to Spengler as a conflict between two historical principles. On one side stood the Confederacy, representing an aristocratic culture rooted in land, honor, and inherited obligation. On the other stood the Union, embodying the advancing civilization of industry, bureaucracy, and mass democracy. The Northern war effort mobilized vast industrial resources, coordinated transportation networks, and centralized political authority with remarkable effectiveness. Armies equipped with modern weaponry moved across territories with mechanical precision, supported by an economic infrastructure capable of sustaining prolonged conflict.

Within this confrontation, Spengler identified figures whose personal character reflected the deeper symbolic meaning of the struggle. Abraham Lincoln emerged as the political figure who gave decisive shape to the ideological language of the Union, elevating the conflict from a constitutional crisis into a struggle framed in moral and universal terms. In his speeches, the preservation of the Union appeared as more than a political necessity; it took on the character of a historical mission, expressed through abstract ideals of liberty, equality, and democratic continuity. In this sense, the Union cause assumed the features of what Carl Schmitt would recognize as a moralized politics, where the enemy is no longer merely opposed but implicitly delegitimized. At the same time, one can discern in this transformation the Spenglerian shift from organic culture to late civilizational form, where living traditions give way to universal claims and expansive systems. Lincoln's later monumentalization—most visibly in the Lincoln Memorial—thus reflects more than commemoration;

it marks the elevation of his figure into a symbol of the Union's abstract, enduring mission, carved into the stone of American historical consciousness.

In contrast, Robert E. Lee appears as the archetype of the tragic aristocratic hero: an expression of a still-living cultural form rather than an ideological construct. Lee's bearing, marked by restraint, dignity, and unwavering loyalty, reflects a world in which authority arises from regality and service rather than abstract doctrine. His command did not rest on proclamations or universal claims, but on an inherited ethos that bound the warrior to the community and duty. In this sense, Lee embodies the final flowering of a cultural aristocracy at the threshold of its dissolution. His campaigns thus take on the character of sacrificial acts, carried out in defense of a form of life already entering its twilight. Against the rising, moralized universalism of the Union—a politics that dissolves concrete distinctions into abstract norms—Lee is a figure of form, limit, and tragic necessity, akin to a classical hero who confronts the irreversible movement of history with composure, fully aware that destiny has already turned against him.

The war itself thus acquired a metaphysical dimension. Battles across Virginia, Pennsylvania, and the Mississippi Valley became expressions of a deeper historical transformation unfolding within Western civilization. Industrial production, centralized administration, and democratic mobilization combined to produce a formidable instrument of modern warfare. The Union's victory signaled the triumph of the civilization principle over the organic culture embodied by the Southern aristocracy. Railways transported troops and supplies with unprecedented efficiency; factories produced weapons in vast quantities; bureaucratic systems coordinated logistics across immense distances.

Spengler interpreted this outcome as part of a larger pattern visible throughout world history. Ancient Greece experienced a similar transition when the vibrant cultural creativity of the classical *polis* yielded to the imperial structures of Rome. The Roman Empire imposed administrative unity and military discipline across the Mediterranean world, establishing a civilization characterized by infrastructure and law. The luminous cultural vitality of Hellenic civilization gradually faded within this imperial behemoth. Spengler regarded the American Civil War as an analogous moment in which an aristocratic culture encountered the ascending forces of modern civilization.

Following the Confederacy's defeat, the United States advanced rapidly towards the characteristics Spengler associated with late civilization. Industrial expansion accelerated, urban populations increased dramatically, and financial institutions gained immense influence over economic life. The federal government extended its administrative authority across wider domains, regulating commerce and social policy. Technological innovations reshaped communication and transportation, linking the continent through integrated networks of production and distribution.

In Spengler's broader philosophy, such developments signified the consolidation of the civilization phase within the Faustian culture of the West. Civilization represents the final stage of a cultural organism's life cycle, characterized by urban concentration, technological mastery, and rationalized governance. Creative energies that once manifested through art, religion, and patrician ideals redirect themselves towards technical innovation and political agitation. The heroic figures of earlier epochs yield to administrators, financiers, and engineers who manage the complex mechanisms of modern society.

Within this interpretation, the memory of the Confederacy acquires symbolic significance. Monuments, battlefields, and historical narratives preserve the image of a society shaped by inherited roles and aristocratic codes. The Confederate flag becomes less a marker of regional politics and more a relic of a cultural form whose vitality belonged to an earlier phase of Western history. The outcome of the war established the direction of American development for generations to come. The Northern industrial order demonstrated the immense organizational power of modern society.

In Spengler's austere vision, the fall of the Confederacy marked a turning point in the historical destiny of the West. The victory of industrial civilization accelerated the transformation of America into a continental power governed by centralized institutions and economic expansion. The older aristocratic ethos receded into historical memory, preserved in literature and regional traditions. Through this transformation, the United States assumed a central role within the final phase of the Faustian world, a civilization of immense dynamism shaped by technology, finance, and political demagogy.

In the fetid twilight of that April in '65, when the last ragged banners of the Confederacy were trampled into the red clay of Appomattox and the final bulwark of traditionalist America—rooted in soil, blood, and elder gods of hearth and kin—shattered like a porcelain mask beneath the grinding maw of the North, there stirred from its grave a thing older than any war: the soulless Yankee machine, vast and cyclopean, forged in the black pits of industry and fed upon the forbidden mathematics of steam and steel. No longer content with its own continent, it uncoiled its iron tentacles across the seas, a warpath of smokestacks and telegraph wires that devoured every ancient rite and whispered custom—the veiled shrines of the East, the drum-haunted groves of Africa, the stone circles of forgotten Europe—until the world itself was rendered into one vast, humming abattoir of progress. From the barred window of his crumbling asylum, old Ezekiel Huckster grabbed my arm with fingers like desiccated roots and hissed through cracked lips, eyes bulging with the sight of things no sane mind should bear: "They fell, boy—the gray ghosts and their old ways—and with them died the last ward against the crawling chaos! Now the machine marches unopposed, grinding every tradition to powder beneath its wheels, and we stand at the threshold of the final age… the age of destructive globalization, where all souls are melted down into identical cogs for its endless, starless hunger!"

14. American Archeofuturism

This chapter draws on Jack Kerouac, Arthur Rimbaud, and Guillaume Faye to sketch an American Archeofuturism, where the search for movement and intensity points beyond the implosion of the present towards new civilizational forms.

Jack Kerouac understood himself as a loyal son of the United States, a wanderer who searched the continent for the hidden pulse of an older America. His books traveled across highways, deserts, and rail yards in pursuit of a mythic realm that he believed still stirred beneath the asphalt of modern industry. Kerouac imagined a return to a primal republic that existed before factories, bureaucracies, and regimented schedules reshaped the continent. In that imagined America, the land stretched wide and unregulated, freedom flowed like wind across plains and mountains, and the individual stood alone before the horizon with absolute independence. The historical record reveals a far more complex reality, yet Kerouac's vision remained powerful precisely because it expressed a longing rather than a literal past. His work proposed a symbolic America where wandering replaced conformity and personal revelation replaced the routines of modern life.

Kerouac carried a Catholic sense of sin, grace, and redemption that shaped how he saw the world and his own restless life. Like Spengler, he saw Western civilization moving towards enfeeblement, its creative force giving way to habit and drift. This produced a tension between faith and decline in him, a longing for purity and meaning set against a deep awareness that the age around him had lost its center. He regarded the modern world with suspicion, especially the expanding machinery of administration, planning, and rational calculation that dominated twentieth-century civilization. Bureaucratic systems, ideological programs, and intellectual abstractions appeared to him as pale substitutes for the immediacy of lived experience. His distrust extended towards types of thought that relied solely upon analytical reasoning. In their place, he championed instinct, spontaneity, and the eruptive force of the will. Movement across the land, improvisational writing, and spiritual intuition offered him a path towards authenticity. He sought inspiration among mystics, jazz musicians, Catholic saints, and romantic poets, all figures who lived according to inner vibrations rather than external discipline.

Among those poets, one figure towered above the rest: Arthur Rimbaud. Kerouac regarded Rimbaud with an intensity that bordered upon identification. The young French visionary who abandoned literature after his early brilliance became for Kerouac a spiritual companion across time. Rimbaud's life of rebellion, ecstatic insight, and restless wandering mirrored the American writer's own search for revelation. Kerouac imagined that the French poet's spirit had somehow migrated across oceans and centuries into his own existence. This identification reinforced his conviction that poetry and vision arise from the unconscious depths of the soul rather than from calculated technique. Through Rimbaud, he encountered the broader current of French Symbolism, a movement that treated language as an instrument capable of evoking hidden realities.

Within that same mythic tradition arose Guillaume Faye, a thinker whose personality and work carried the intensity of prophetic insight. Faye cultivated a reputation that defied the image of the austere intellectual. He drank heavily, smoked constantly, and moved through life with an appetite for excess that recalled the bohemian circles of nineteenth-century Paris. Participation in pornographic cinema, a restless pursuit of romantic encounters, and an unabashed embrace of sensual experience formed part of his personal mythology. Yet these traits coexisted with a remarkable intellectual productivity. Faye wrote essays, manifestos, and philosophical speculations with relentless energy, seeking to diagnose the destiny of Europe in the age of technological transformation.

Observers often compared Guillaume Faye to the great Symbolist poets of France. The sequence runs from Paul Verlaine and Rimbaud to the dark imagination of Charles Baudelaire, whose vision of modernity fused beauty with decay and insight with disquiet. Baudelaire wrote of the modern city as a place where brilliance and corruption coexist, his tone marked by a persistent pessimism about the direction of the age. Faye shared this intensity of perception and this drive to penetrate beneath appearances. He treated writing as an instrument of revelation. His texts move between political analysis, cultural diagnosis, and a heightened, almost eschatological mode of expression. He formulates axioms about European destiny, anticipates technological upheaval, and seeks to grasp the deeper structure of history as it unfolds.

Faye's central concept, Archeofuturism, gathers these elements into a single vision. He describes a civilization moving through crises towards a synthesis of extremes. On one side is advanced technology, rapid innovation, and scientific power. On the other is the archaic: hierarchy, identity, myth, and rooted community. Archeofuturism rejects the idea that progress requires the abandonment of tradition. Instead, it proposes a future in which technological acceleration coexists with strong cultural archetypes. This idea finds a clear expression in the United States, where a double movement unfolds across the same terrain. Towers of code rise from Silicon Valley, systems of data reshape time, and innovation advances with relentless speed. Yet, beneath this forward motion, another current gathers force. Questions of identity, belonging, and continuity return with increasing urgency. Society speaks in two registers at once: one oriented towards expansion and abstraction, the other towards memory and form, *ethnos* and *ethos*.

Archeofuturism reads this tension as structural rather than accidental. The digital order dissolves boundaries, compresses distance, and reorganizes human life into networks and flows. At the same time, communities seek anchoring points, symbols, and inherited forms that resist this dissolution. The American frontier reappears in a new shape. Expansion continues, yet it moves both outward into technological space and inward towards historical depth. The builder of machines and the seeker of origins begin to converge. Steel and memory, code and lineage, acceleration and continuity form a single field of experience. In this sense, America becomes a testing ground for the Archeofuturist condition, where the future intensifies and the past acquires renewed weight.

The connection between Faye and Baudelaire reveals both affinity and divergence. Baudelaire beheld modernity as a slow descent into splintered forms and drained spirit, a glittering ruin where brilliance flickers amidst corpses. His vision moves through shadow and perfume, steeped in a lucid melancholy, sensing within the very pulse of modern life the quiet germ of dissolution, a sweetness already touched by rot, a radiance haunted by its own undoing. Faye discerns the same dark currents yet refuses their fatal languor, turning the tremor of catastrophes into a threshold of metamorphosis, where the ruins of old forms ignite the birth of sharper, more intense configurations. Both minds move attuned to the secret tides beneath the visible world, each rejecting the mask of appearances, each tracing the hidden logic of their age. Yet where Charles Baudelaire lingers within the perfume of decay, suspended in exquisite tension, Guillaume Faye drives forward with a harder vision, projecting beyond the fracture towards a renewed figure of civilization. In his work, Europe passes through fire and disarray, only to gather itself again in a more condensed, more luminous, and more formidable form.

Faye's temperament reflected the exuberance and volatility associated with the Symbolist tradition. The poets of that movement often embraced extreme experiences in order to break through the boundaries of conventional perception. Absinthe, nocturnal wanderings, and feverish creative bursts formed part of their routines. Faye's life resembled this pattern. He appeared possessed by a relentless drive to uncover new truths and articulate them with striking clarity. His predictions concerning geopolitics, technological acceleration, and cultural transformation sometimes carried a hallucinatory quality, as though they emerged from a vision glimpsed through flashes of lightning. In contrast with Baudelaire's darker meditations on the putrefaction of modernity, Faye frequently expressed a fierce optimism regarding the possibilities of the future. He spoke of the coming era of rapid technological progress with enthusiasm, imagining laboratories where scientists might even create hybrid forms of life through advanced genetic engineering.

This charged atmosphere of visionary speculation binds the European Symbolists to the wandering mysticism that set Jack Kerouac in motion across the American expanse. In both vectors, imagination becomes an instrument of penetration, a blade drawn against the dull surface of the visible world, seeking entry into deeper strata of meaning. The poet, the seer, the restless traveler assume the role of mediator, translating obscure signals from hidden realities into fleeting glimpses within ordinary perception. Jack Kerouac's highways unfurl like burning veins across the country, while Guillaume Faye's manifestos strike with declarative force; each, in his own register, channels the same fevered impulse to rupture appearances and expose the concealed skeleton of modern civilization.

The narrative voice that emerges from these reflections often takes on the character of a wandering consciousness moving through landscapes charged with memory and myth. One might imagine a solitary figure walking along a gravel path towards a weathered shack standing in the middle of a vast cornfield. The horizon stretches outward in silent symmetry, the wind rustles through dry stalks, and the imagination drifts towards distant continents and forgotten histories. The mind fills with images of Africa's interior landscapes, of drums echoing across savannas, of explorers and traders who once crossed deserts in pursuit of fortune or revelation. Memories arrive as fragments, as though filtered through a sieve that allows only scattered impressions to remain.

In this visionary reverie, time collapses into layers. A season spent in Ethiopia returns through flashes of recollection: the glare of the equatorial sun, the dust rising beneath caravan hooves, the sting of injury in a wounded knee that refuses to heal. The wound festers beneath the skin like an abscess, a physical reminder of the friction between civilization and primal existence. The modern world with its traffic fumes and media spectacles appears suddenly fragile, a thin crust stretched over deeper geological strata of human experience. Beneath the surface lie older epochs: Bronze Age settlements, Stone Age migrations, and the primordial struggles of early mankind.

The vista behind the wanderer rises into a barren

plateau where scattered stones form silent monuments to vanished ages. Bones buried beneath layers of sand record the passage of countless generations. Each stratum marks another stage in the long evolution of civilization. At the far edge of imagination stands a solitary black monolith, erect against the desert sky like a witness shaped from eternity. Around it, early humans once fought over scraps of meat abandoned by the ancestors of modern predators. In that distant moment, the entire arc of human history began its ascent from instinct towards culture.

15. Speak Free or Die

This chapter contrasts the American defense of free speech with the increasingly regulated discourse of Europe, examining how the management and criminalization of expression signals a deeper transformation within Western civilization.

Charlie Kirk sends the warning like a broadcast cut through static, signal crossing the Atlantic into Europe. Once a zone of argument, heresy, and voices colliding in open air. Now the tone shifts. Words hit filters. Speech meets checkpoints, clerks, codes, silent edits. Files move. Permissions required. A sentence triggers a process. The system listens. Europe stands as the exhibit. A civilization that forged rebellion now routes speech through procedure. Debate becomes managed output. Language passes through screens, guidelines, and compliance grids. The citizen speaks inside a structure that measures, flags, and redirects. Authority moves from voice to apparatus. From man to system. From speech to criminal codes.

The history of Europe once displayed a very different spirit. The continent produced the Protestant Reformation, an upheaval in which figures such as Martin Luther openly challenged ecclesiastical authority through pamphlets, sermons, and public debate. Luther's ninety-five theses spread across Germany through printing presses and public discussion. Princes, scholars, and common citizens argued openly about theology and political authority. The result transformed the religious and political structure of Europe. In the following centuries, Europe produced the Enlightenment, when philosophers such as Voltaire attacked censorship and defended the right to criticize power. Voltaire's writings ridiculed monarchy, church institutions, and dogmatic authority with sharp satire. Pamphlets circulated across France and Britain. Coffeehouses filled with debates about religion, government, and philosophy. The European tradition once celebrated bold speech as a force capable of overturning old regimes.

Charlie Kirk maps a new grid over Europe. Public life rewired. Speech routed through systems. Laws spread like circuitry across states. Words no longer travel free. They pass through scanners, silent flags in the background. The old arena of argument turns into a managed zone. Every phrase carries a risk profile.

Germany runs tight protocols. Symbols tagged, meanings fixed, deviations logged. The law draws lines around history and marks certain signs as forbidden signals. Then comes *NetzDG: a* rapid-response mechanism. Platforms act as enforcers. Content flagged as illegal must vanish fast. Hours, not days. The machine does not wait. Companies scan, filter, and delete to avoid penalties. Private networks become extensions of state oversight. Algorithms and compliance teams replace open dispute. Across the channel, Britain activates Communications Act 2003. Messages judged "offensive" or "improper" trigger investigation. A post, a joke, a comment—pulled into legal review. Language itself enters the docket. France adds another layer. Speech tied to history and ethnic identity moves inside regulated boundaries. Certain historical interpretations permitted, others restricted. The past becomes a managed archive.

Officials speak of "stability," of "preventing extremism," of "keeping the peace." The language sounds clean.

The effect runs deeper. Critics read a pattern. Authority migrates. From the individual speaker to the administrative system. From open exchange to supervised output. The border of speech shifts inward. Not a visible wall. A field of invisible constraints. The system learns, adjusts, tightens. Speech continues. Yet always inside the grid.

Kirk's warning rests upon a contrast with the historical traditions of the United States. American political culture grew within a society that placed extraordinary emphasis upon open speech. The First Amendment of the American Constitution declares that Congress shall make no law abridging the freedom of speech or of the press. This principle formed the backbone of American public life from the early republic onward. Newspapers in the nineteenth century attacked presidents, political parties, and government institutions with remarkable ferocity. Editors wrote pamphlets accusing rivals of corruption, incompetence, and treason. Public argument often reached intense levels, yet the legal system protected the right to speak.

Examples from American history demonstrate the importance of this tradition. During the American Revolution, pamphleteers such as Thomas Paine circulated texts that challenged the authority of the British crown. Paine's *Common Sense* argued openly for independence and attacked monarchy in blunt, direct language that reached farmers, merchants, and soldiers across the colonies. This took place before the First Amendment existed. There was no formal protection for free speech, and such writing could be treated as sedition or treason under British law. Yet the revolutionary cause spread through words printed on cheap paper and carried into taverns, churches, and public squares. Open political argument emerged in practice before it was secured in law, and the First Amendment later formalized a freedom that had already been exercised.

In *Common Sense*, Paine cuts the sentence down to

bone and nerve: society rises from desire, from need, from the pull of one body towards another, a field of attraction where lives knot together and warmth circulates. Government enters from another origin, a colder birth, shaped by vice, by the dark impulses that require restraint. Society binds, gathers, intensifies contact; government separates, marks, divides. One moves like a current of life, a patron of connection and shared existence; the other stands as correction, a punisher that presses limits against the restless edges of human conduct.

The same pattern continued in later decades. Abraham Lincoln engaged in a famous series of public debates with Stephen A. Douglas during the campaign of 1858. These debates drew large crowds who listened to long speeches addressing the future of slavery and the meaning of the Union. Political disagreement unfolded openly before thousands of citizens. Newspapers published transcripts so readers across the country could examine the arguments themselves. The debates demonstrated a civic culture that trusted the people to evaluate competing ideas.

The twentieth century produced additional examples. During the Vietnam War protests, American citizens gathered in massive demonstrations criticizing the policies of their own government. Students marched through Washington, journalists exposed military controversies, and political leaders faced fierce public scrutiny. Courts repeatedly defended the right of protest and speech even during periods of national tension. The American system treated disagreement as part of democratic vitality rather than as a threat requiring administrative control.

Kirk therefore interprets Europe's present environment as a reversal of the historical pattern that once defined Western civilization. The continent that generated the bold voices of the Reformation and Enlightenment now operates through expanding regulatory structures governing speech and expression. European governments often justify these measures through the catchphrases of "public safety" and "social harmony." Yet the effect, according to critics, includes a narrowing of permissible discourse and a growing role for government institutions in determining acceptable opinion.

The contrast between past and present is nowhere more plainly seen than in the visible form of Europe itself. The monuments of earlier ages still stand in full view, bearing witness to the spirit that once animated the continent. Notre-Dame Cathedral rises above the Seine as a lasting emblem of religious conviction and the ambition of the truly soulful medieval mind. The Palace of Westminster reflects a long history of public deliberation and the gradual shaping of constitutional government. Institutions such as the University of Oxford preserve traditions of learning that extend across centuries, connecting the present generation with the labors of those who came before.

Yet, when one turns from these enduring structures to the present condition of public life, a different scene appears. The activity of politics now centers less upon open debate and more upon bureaucratic processes. Committees, regulations, and legal provisions occupy the ground once held by vigorous discussion. The regulation of speech, especially within the domains of media and digital communication, has become a matter of formal oversight. Thus the same continent that produced courageous expressions of faith and inquiry now devotes increasing attention to the management and limitation of expression. The contrast is evident to any observer willing to compare what remains with what now prevails.

Kirk's argument extends beyond policy into the deeper question of civilizational confidence. A society that encourages open debate demonstrates trust in its own cultural resilience. Competing voices enter the public arena and attempt to persuade citizens through argument and evidence. That process produces friction, controversy, and passionate disagreement. Yet it also generates intellectual dynamism. The American experience illustrates how fierce public argument can coexist with political stability across long periods of history.

The alternative model, in Kirk's view, emphasizes precaution and regulation. Governments intervene to manage speech before conflicts *might* emerge. Government institutions evaluate expressions that *might* provoke "offense" or "social tension." Over time, such systems will encourage caution among citizens who prefer silence over legal or professional risk. Public debate gradually moves from crowded squares and newspapers towards narrower channels supervised by experts and regulatory boards.

Kirk's message ultimately concerns the direction of Western civilization as a whole. Europe and the United States share deep historical roots. The political philosophy of the American Founding Fathers drew heavily upon European traditions of law, religion, and philosophy. The warning therefore addresses a common inheritance. If the institutions of open speech weaken on one side of the Atlantic, the consequences may eventually reach the other side as well.

In Kirk's imagery, the situation resembles a torch carried across generations. Earlier Europeans lit the flame through revolutions of thought and speech. American institutions preserved that flame through constitutional protections and a culture of vigorous debate. The present moment demands renewed attention to that tradition. The lesson drawn from history remains clear: civilizations that protect open speech preserve their capacity for renewal, while societies that restrict expression risk replacing the energy of public argument with totalitarian supervision where war is peace and freedom is slavery ad nauseam.

A hard, electric glare flooded the square, every surface scrubbed clean and watched, and he spoke without turning his head, lips barely moving, "You feel it, yes? The pressure on the tongue." Loudspeakers bled a steady stream of approved phrases, clipped and certain, each word marching in lockstep: safety, values, cohesion. "They have reduced the language," he said, voice thin as wire, "cut it down to size so that only the permitted shapes remain." I tried to form a reply, yet the words stalled, as if passing through a sieve. "And what slips through?" I asked. He gave a dry, humorless breath. "Nothing that matters. Anything outside the frame draws attention. Anything that names too clearly, compares too sharply, or remembers too far—flagged, recorded, punished." A patrol passed, boots measured, faces blank, and the screens flickered with reminders of rules recited as if they were facts of nature. "They say it is protection," he continued, "yet protection here means restriction. They say it is order, yet order here means narrowing." The phrases sounded again, louder now, until they seemed to press against the skull. "You see the design," he said, finally turning, eyes fixed and unblinking. "First they train you to speak in their terms. Then they forbid what remains. In time, the forbidden thought withers, and the permitted word stands alone." I felt the weight of it settle, a closing system, seamless and complete, where language no longer served the speaker, and where every sentence carried the quiet risk of crossing a line drawn everywhere and nowhere at once.

16. Cimmerian America

This chapter draws on Patrick J. Buchanan and the figure of Conan the Barbarian to confront the death of the West as both an ending and a threshold. It considers whether collapse marks finality or the beginning of a new civilizational cycle shaped by struggle and will.

Beneath a sky of burnished bronze, where the wind moaned through shattered towers and the bones of empires lay half-buried in dust, a lone chronicler set down his warning. His name was Patrick J. Buchanan, and his scroll about the demise of the Occident read less like a scholar's treatise than a doom-song recited beside a dying king. No sorcery stained its pages, no demon's name inked in blood, yet every line carried the weight of prophecy, as though some grim seer had glimpsed the twilight of a mighty realm.

"I have walked the ruins before they were ruins," Buchanan seemed to murmur through the parchment, "and I tell you, no empire falls in a day. The fall begins in the soul."

In elder ages, the West had risen like a barbarian warlord from the mist: young, fierce, and unyielding. From the storm-lashed coasts of Europe to the vast, untamed reaches of the American frontier, men whipped order from chaos with iron and will. Kingdoms rose beneath banners soaked in blood and glory. Cathedrals thrust skyward like spears hurled at the heavens. The minds of philosophers rang like hammer blows upon the anvil of truth, while caravels cut through unknown seas, their sails swollen with destiny. It was an age of sinew and fire, where faith and ambition marched as one.

"A people with children and faith fears neither winter nor war," growled an imagined chieftain in Buchanan's vision. "Their line endures, and their gods walk beside them."

Yet Buchanan's gaze, keen as a hunter's, pierced beyond the golden legends into the creeping dusk of later years. The foes he named bore no shields, no swords. They came as a predator comes: slow, patient, and unseen. In the hearths of the West, fewer children were born. Cradles stood empty, gathering dust where once they had rocked with laughter and life. The bloodlines of ancient peoples thinned like a warband dwindling after endless campaigns.

"A fortress may stand tall," Buchanan warned, "yet if no sons rise to guard its walls, its fate is sealed long before the enemy arrives."

While the blood of the old tribes waned, the gates of the cities stood open. From distant lands came multitudes: strangers bearing other tongues, other gods, other memories. They did not storm the walls with ladders and fire; they entered by the roads of labor and refuge, settling like sediment within the ancient streets. Markets filled with foreign wares, and the murmur of unfamiliar speech was heard where once a single voice had spoken.

In a dim hall lit by flickering torches, one might imagine a grizzled veteran speaking to a young warrior:

"The city is still ours," said the youth.

"Aye," the old man replied, staring into the fire, "yet listen closely. Do you still hear your fathers in its streets?"

Buchanan saw also the changing of the West's spirit. Where once the bards sang of heroes, sacrifice, and destiny, a different song now drifted through the halls of culture. Stories splintered into shards. Art twisted into shapes that mocked the old forms. Music lost its harmony and wandered into strange, restless tones. It was as though the spirit of the people had turned inward, questioning itself, doubting its own myths.

"A civilization that forgets its heroes," Buchanan's voice seemed to undulate, "forgets how to become heroic."

Even the sacred fires dimmed. Churches that had once thundered with hymns now stood half-empty, their vast arches confirming absence. The old faith—once the backbone of law, custom, and daily life—yielded ground to a world of shifting beliefs and uncertain truths. The temples still stood, grand as ever, yet their altars felt colder, their flame diminished.

"The gods depart quietly," murmured a priest in the shadow of a crumbling sanctuary. "Only later do men notice the chill."

In the courts of power, a new kind of order arose: vast, intricate, and impersonal. Bureaucracies spread like a maze no man could fully grasp. Scroll upon scroll, decree upon decree, until governance itself became a machine of endless motion. Stability was guaranteed, aye, but at a cost. The fierce independence of the old citizen gave way to the managed life of the subject, guided by unseen hands.

Buchanan's vision took the shape of a mighty kingdom whose towers still gleamed in the sun, whose armies remained unmatched, whose wealth surpassed that of all ages past. Yet beneath its marble halls, hairline fractures spread through the foundation.

"The danger," he wrote, "comes not from the battering ram, but from the slow forgetting of who we are."

Still, his tale did not end in desolation. For in the dim memory of the West burned a spark older than any empire: a barbarian fire that no decadence could wholly extinguish. As Conan of Cimmeria rose from chains and exile through sheer will, so too did the spirit of renewal persist.

"Steel your hearts," a voice seemed to cry from the ages. "For kingdoms fall, yet men endure, and from the ashes, strength is forged anew."

Buchanan held that the West still possessed vast reserves of strength: its myth-making power, its instinct for order, and its capacity to shape the unknown. The same spirit that had crossed oceans and touched the stars still stirred beneath the surface, awaiting those bold enough to awaken it.

So the chronicle closes upon a windswept battlement. The past lies behind like a field of victories: Renaissance, revolution, discovery. Before stretches the long, uncertain road into the shadow that is called the future. In the great hall, the warriors gather, their faces lit by firelight. Outside, the night deepens.

One turns to another and asks, "Is this the end?"

The answer comes, low and steady: "That depends on whether we still remember how to fight."

17. Exoteric Trumpism

Exoteric Trumpism strides under harsh light, skin peeled back, nerves exposed, every motion recorded in the open air of consequence. It stands across from Esoteric Trumpism, which moved through charged symbols, hidden correspondences, and prophetic expectation. There, Trump rose as Caesar, summoned from the fatigue of a civilization that had forgotten command. He appeared as the breaker of fossilized forms, the restorer of rank, and the voice of destiny cutting through the soft rot of procedure and consensus. He carried the image of the redeemer, the one who would gather scattered energies, bind them into order, and drive them forward with force.

That vision grew from the deeper evolution of cultures, the old cycle moving through awakening, flowering, and hardening. In the late hour, the shell remains while the core drains away. Parliaments rattle with hollow speech. Markets pulse where the spirit once lived. The masses drift, detached from origin, hungry for direction, craving authority that strikes clean and holds. Into that vacuum steps the man of decision, the figure who does not argue, does not hesitate, and shapes reality through will. In *Esoteric Trumpism* (2024), Trump seemed to step into that role. His tone cut against consensus. His presence disrupted the smooth language of liberal management. His gestures carried the scent of rupture. A Caesar in outline, a redeemer in formation, a signal that the long drift might finally come to an end.

The promise formed with force and clarity. America would return to itself, not as an abstraction, not as a mere market, but as an authentic people grounded in identity and continuity. Money would again kneel before power. Borders would close with finality, not as a policy but as an act. The state would serve its own, shaped by the memory of the ancestors and driven by destiny. The image burned with intensity: a decisive stroke, a reordering, a new phase rising from the ruins of liberal collapse. In that image, Trump the redeemer stood ready, hand on the lever of history.

Then the scene breaks open. The esoteric dissolves into the exoteric. The figure steps out of symbols into the field of actions, where every gesture leaves a trace and every decision coalesces into a consequence. The system waits, immense, adaptive, layered with interests, networks, and habits formed over decades. It does not collapse. It absorbs.

The war with Iran erupts as the first great test, and it unfolds like a fevered landscape of bodies, heat, metal, and dust. Night skies pulse with missiles cutting arcs through black air, sirens tearing through cities, fragments of steel falling into streets and roofs and flesh. Drones circle like insects over desert and concrete, their hum constant, intimate, invasive. Explosions open the ground, tear buildings into raw shapes, scatter limbs, blood, smoke, cries swallowed by engines and fire. The Strait chokes, oil slicks spread, flames rise from tankers, water burns, air thickens with chemical taste. Official voices speak of precision, of targets, of victory measured in strikes. On the ground, the scene dissolves into fragments: bodies carried, bodies counted, bodies unnamed. The war expands in pulses, each strike answered, each answer widening the field. Objectives shift, language shifts, yet the movement continues, restless, uncontrolled. Victory is declared, repeated, amplified, while deployments grow, while costs rise, while the structure strains under its own extension.

In this terrain, the Caesar should appear as clarity, as direction cutting through chaos, as will imposing form. Instead, motion multiplies and direction disperses. The war becomes a surface of sensation, of impact, of endless reaction, a cycle feeding itself. Markets tremble, currencies slide, supply lines twist and snap. The empire stretches across distance and heat, chasing a shape it cannot hold. Momentum carries on, yet purpose dissolves. The conflict becomes a mirror of late might: vast, violent, unformed, and unable to close.

Trump sought unipolarity, sought the restoration of American hegemony through force, through demonstration, through domination of space and resource. The war was meant as an assertion. It becomes acceleration of the opposite. The conflict pushes states towards autonomy, alternative alignments, and distance from Washington's orbit. Multipolarity hardens through the very act meant to suppress it. The strike meant to restore singular power disperses power across many centers.

Immigration is the second stage, the promise of a decisive act rooted in the land itself. The image held force: mass deportation, a clean stroke, a boundary drawn with finality, a people restored through separation and clarity. Crowds imagined movement, trains, planes, lines of return, and a redefinition of the political body. In practice, the scene breaks down. Raids occur, removals proceed, files circulate, courts intervene, orders pause, restart, narrow, expand. Each action meets a counteraction, each decree meets a procedure. The great act disintegrates into a chain of partial gestures, each bounded, each absorbed. Numbers rise, then stall, then shift. Categories define action: criminals, cases, exceptions. The total vision shrinks into a maze of files and decrees. The structure, hostile to heritage Americans, remains: layered, resistant, and intact.

Within the movement, another transformation unfolds, quieter at first, then sharp. MAGA begins as a chant and unity, a call directed inward, a signal of return and restoration. Over time, another phrase emerges, first as murmur, then as accusation: MIGA–"Make Israel Great Again." The shift marks perception, a sense that direction bends outward, that energy flows towards commitments shaped beyond the nation. Israel stands at the center of this perception, especially as the war intensifies, as policy aligns, as resources flow, as language frames the conflict in terms that extend beyond immediate national interest. The base feels the strain. Voices divide. Some affirm the alignment as strength, as necessity within a broader field. Others see deviation, a fracture cutting through the original unity, a redirection of will towards external ends.

The language of sovereignty continues, firm, resonant, repeated across platforms and speeches. Action traces another pattern. Donor networks pulse beneath policy. The system remains, flexible, redirecting force. The figure who stood as breaker moves within this web, guided, constrained, shaped. The Caesar image thins, flickers, gives way to a role within the established order Trump was meant to overturn.

This is the moment of exposure. Exoteric Trumpism names this condition, this stripping away of symbols under the weight of actions. The redeemer image warps into the record of decisions, into wars that spread, into policies that splinter, into movements that divide. Gestures replace transformation. Conflicts loop back into continuity. The system bends, adapts, and persists.

The philosophical weight settles deeper. A Caesar emerges through acts that alter structure, through will that reshapes the distribution of power in lasting form. He stands above networks, breaks them, redirects them, imposes a new order that holds beyond momentary shock.

Words cannot summon him. Desire cannot create him. He appears through incisive section and tenacious retention, through decisions that reconfigure the field.

Trump is situated within this inversion as the exoteric failure of the hoped-for Caesar. He bore the morbid symptom of crisis, articulated the appetite for decisive intervention, and effected the fixation of return, identity, and sovereignty. He entered the field, moved through it, and left the structure standing. The myth burns out, the reality remains: a leader within the system, shaped by its currents, reflecting its limits. The age continues in its winter, the air sharp, the forms hardened, the sense of ending mixed with the pressure of beginning. The call for decision grows louder, the need for form more intense. Somewhere within this pressure, the conditions gather for a figure who will act with clarity, who will impose direction that endures, who will break the structures that bind the present. Until that figure appears, the distinction holds with force: esoteric vision on one side, exoteric reality on the other, and between them the lesson carved into history, a promise that rose with brilliance and settled into lame duck continuity.

The night gathers over the broken horizon like a sentient weight, pressing down upon the cities and deserts alike, and in that dim interval between siren and silence a voice emerges—thin, strained, yet possessed of a dreadful certainty—"Do you hear it?" he asks, turning towards me with eyes that seem to reflect a light that has no source, "not the explosions, not the engines, but the pattern beneath them, the melody that repeats." I answer with hesitation, for the air itself hums with something deeper than machinery, something ancient that stirs beneath the language of policy and war. "It is only the conflict," I say, though the words fall flat, lifeless, unable to hold their ground. He shakes his head slowly, as if correcting a child. "Conflict serves as the surface," he says, "yet beneath it moves a geometry of collapse, a design that unfolds whether men will it or resist it." The distant flashes return, not as isolated bursts, but as a sequence, a code impressed upon the dark, and in that moment the structures of power, the speeches, the declarations of strength all appear as thin veils stretched over something vast and indifferent. "The empire believes it acts," he continues, voice tightening, "yet it is being acted through, its will a conduit for forces it cannot name." I attempt to respond, to assert some remnant of agency, yet the words refuse formation, for the ground beneath thought itself begins to shift. "Then what remains?" I ask at last. He leans closer, and his voice drops into a tone that seems older than the language he uses. "Only this," he says, "that every figure who rises as a redeemer must pass through this revelation, that power without understanding becomes the instrument of its own undoing." The sirens return, louder now, yet they seem distant, irrelevant, as if belonging to another layer of reality. "And Trump?" I ask, though I already sense the answer forming beyond speech. A faint, almost sorrowful expression crosses his face. "He believed himself the wielder," he replies, "yet he stands among the wielded, a shape moving within a pattern that neither begins nor ends with him." The sky flickers again, though now the light reveals less than it conceals, and as the sound deepens into a continuous, low vibration, I begin to understand that what unfolds before us is neither victory nor defeat, but the slow, inevitable unveiling of a structure far older than any nation, far colder than any ambition, a structure in which every act, every war, every proclamation feeds into a design that waits, patient and complete, for those who mistake motion for mastery.